JAPANESE TEAPOTS

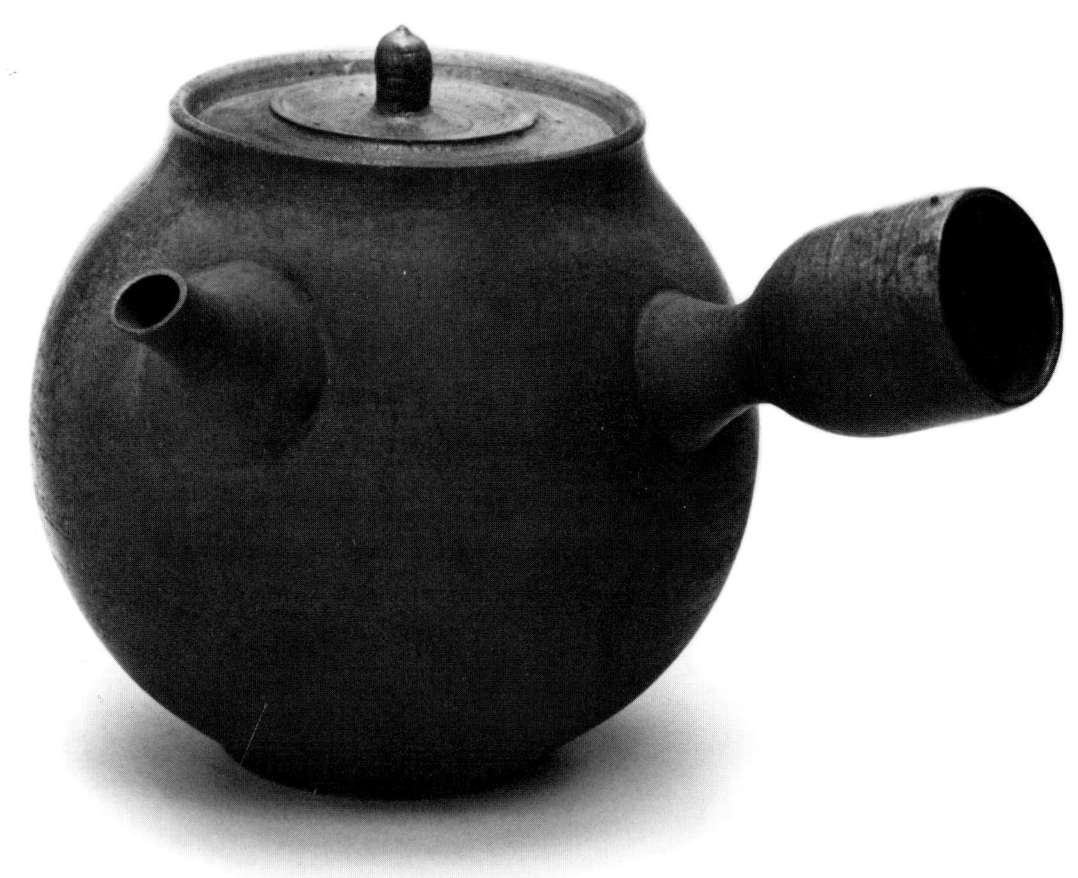

Form and Function series

JAPANESE TEAPOTS

text by Noritake Kanzaki
photographs by Kiyomi Suganuma

in collaboration with the
Japan Research Institute for Tourism and Cultural Resources

Kodansha International
Tokyo, New York, San Francisco

distributed
in the United States
by Kodansha International/USA Ltd.,
through Harper & Row, Publishers, Inc.,
10 East 53rd Street, New York, New York 10022.

published
by Kodansha International Ltd.,
12–21 Otowa 2-chome, Bunkyo-ku, Tokyo 112
and Kodansha International/USA Ltd.,
10 East 53rd Street, New York, New York 10022
and 44 Montgomery Street, San Francisco, California 94104.

printed in Japan

first edition, 1981

LCC 78–71255
ISBN 0–87011–392–5
JBC 2372–787626–2361

Japanese Teapots

Noritake Kanzaki

There are two types of teapot in Japan. One is a larger, traditionally Japanese pot (*dobin*), once used for decocting medicinal herbal infusions and, later, to steep low-grade tea. The second is a small teapot (*kyūsu*), introduced from China, for drinking higher quality tea. Generally speaking, the large type of teapot is an earthenware receptacle with a round body, a spout, a lid, and a semicircular handle.

The earliest antecedents of the larger type of teapot so far excavated date from about 1500 B.C., are of unglazed earthenware, and conform to an archetypal "teapot shape." What they were used for, however, is far from clear. In the protohistoric and early historical periods of Japanese history, up to about A.D. 700, an unglazed earthenware known as Hajiki ware became the prevalent style of pottery. Certain Hajiki pots have traces of soot around their base and so were presumably placed on a fire to boil water. These pots bear a distinct resemblance to the modern teapot. Only a few of them, however, have been excavated. Since in those days tea drinking had not reached Japanese shores, and the purity of the water was high enough to make boiling unnecessary, it seems unlikely that there was much need in everyday life for a vessel of this sort.

We are not yet in a position to tell with any degree of certainty what these pots were for, but they may well have been used for brewing herbal medicines. Partly under the influence of practices in Korea and China, the drying, brewing, and drinking of various herbs became popular in Japan to cure all sorts of diseases. In fact, tea first was regarded as an elixir by the Buddhist monks who introduced the drink from China. The practice of decocting medicinal herbs in unglazed earthenware teapots still survives nowadays, and such teapots are sold in the pharmacies that dispense traditional oriental medicaments. Despite the fact that modern saucepans and well-made kettles can be bought easily in the shops, people continue to use these rather primitive teapots for medicinal purposes. No doubt this is due to some extent to the medicinal properties ascribed to the pots themselves, but it also reflects how deep-rooted the practice is.

From medieval times on, unglazed earthenware pots began to be used for tea. It was mainly among Buddhist monks, in court circles, and among other members of the upper strata of society that the custom of drinking tea first spread. In the case of powdered tea, water heated in the pot was poured directly into a teabowl, while with normal green tea it was poured into a smaller pot containing the tea leaves. But already in those days several types of iron hot-water kettles existed, and it should not be thought that the earthenware pots alone were used to heat water.

Not until the seventeenth century did the use of unglazed earthenware pots become widespread. It was a different way of drinking tea, deriving directly from the practice of brewing medicinal herbs, that brought about this change. Chiefly in Edo and Kyoto, the two principal cities of Japan at this time, and among the merchants and craftsmen of these cities, it became an everyday custom to drink tea made from a lower grade of tea leaves, which were dried but not treated. As with medicinal herbs, the water was heated with the tea leaves in the same pot. Lower grade tea is often prepared in this way nowadays and drunk after a meal.

In the countryside, however, a considerable number of people, especially farmers in north and east Japan, largely because of the difficulties involved in cultivating the tea plant in a cool climate, drank not tea but plain hot water after their meals. In south and west Japan, on the other hand, country people drank a concoction known as "mountain tea," consisting of leaves from the willow tree mixed with leaves from tea bushes growing wild. And there may well have been other yet stranger variations. In fact, it was not really until the middle of the last century, when Japan began the process of modernization, that the habit of drinking low-quality tea (*bancha*) served from a ceramic teapot really caught on among people in all parts of Japan, and teapots of all types—unglazed earthenware, glazed stoneware, and porcelain teapots—became common household objects.

Glazed stoneware and porcelain teapots are stronger than unglazed earthenware teapots, the firing temperature and density of the clay bodies being higher, so that they become good conductors of heat. Such pots are, however, liable to crack if placed directly over a fire. Adding a glaze has increased the strength of pots, but has meant a change in the way *bancha* tea is prepared. Nowadays, the tea leaves are normally put into a stoneware or porcelain teapot; the water is heated in a separate vessel, poured into the teapot, and the tea is ready to be served after a few minutes' steeping.

The large sort of teapot (*dobin*) is not only used for tea and herbs; it can be used to prepare a dish known as *dobin-mushi*, or "teapot steaming." *Dobin-mushi* consists of mushrooms, chicken, fish, and vegetables cut up and sliced, put in a teapot, and then steamed inside the pot over a naked flame. Originally this dish contained only mushrooms, which were cooked in the teapot, and this is why unglazed earthenware teapots are still known as mushroom pots (*naba dobin*) in parts of Japan.

The small sort of Japanese teapot (*kyūsu*), unlike its larger brother, has always been used as a vessel for tea. It is not only smaller in size, but has a different sort of handle, a grip like the handle of a small saucepan attached roughly at right angles to the spout. Otherwise the two sorts of teapot are basically similar. The small teapot is normally used for high- or medium-grade tea. The tea leaves are first put into the teapot, and hot water is poured onto them. After a minute or two of steeping, the tea is ready. Recently, low grade tea has come to be prepared frequently in *kyūsu*, even though these pots were originally intended for tea at least one notch up from the lower grades.

The custom of drinking medium- and high-quality tea was initially cultivated by the literati of Ming dynasty China, and, together with the small teapot itself, was exported to Japan probably some time in the sixteenth or seventeenth century. According to one story, it was first introduced by the Chinese priest Ingen, founder of the Ōbaku sect of Zen Buddhism, who arrived in Japan in 1654.

A typical *kyūsu* is made of a reddish brown clay, is unglazed, but is incised with a Chinese poem and a landscape with mountains and a river. Japanese pottery is notable for the smoothness of its surfaces, and these incised decorations represent an exception, which can be accounted for by the fact that the *kyūsu* was a cultural import from China. It is, in fact, quite different in form from traditional Japanese objects.

Some of the kilns still actively producing teapots are:

Large teapots (*dobin*):	Aizu-Hongō	Fukushima Prefecture
	Mashiko	Tochigi Prefecture
	Shigaraki	Shiga Prefecture
	Kiyomizu	Kyoto
Small teapots (*kyūsu*):	Aizu-Hongō	Fukushima Prefecture
	Sōma	Fukushima Prefecture
	Seto	Aichi Prefecture
	Tokoname	Aichi Prefecture
	Banko	Mie Prefecture
	Kutani	Ishikawa Prefecture
	Hagi	Yamaguchi Prefecture
	Bizen	Okayama Prefecture
	Arita	Saga Prefecture

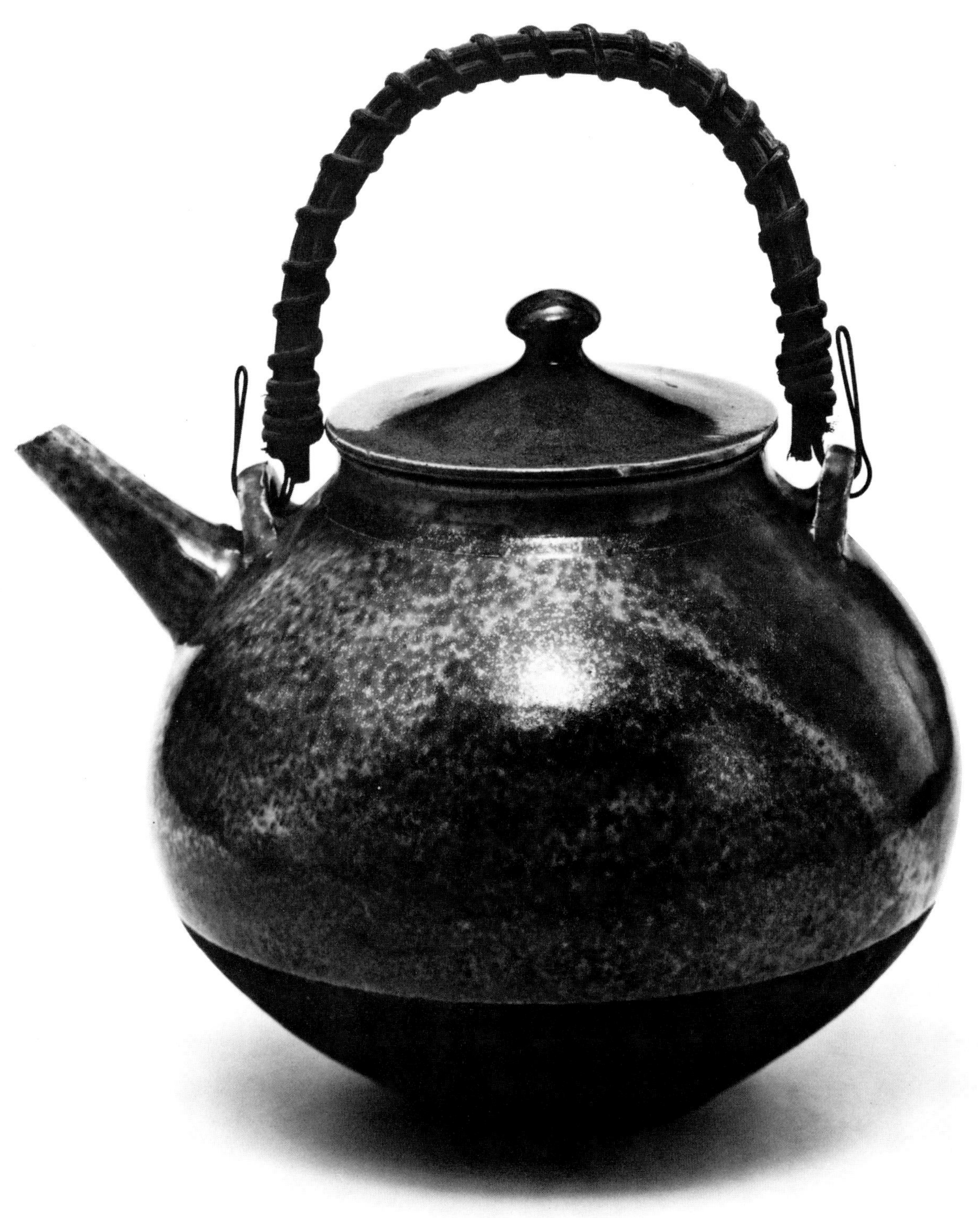

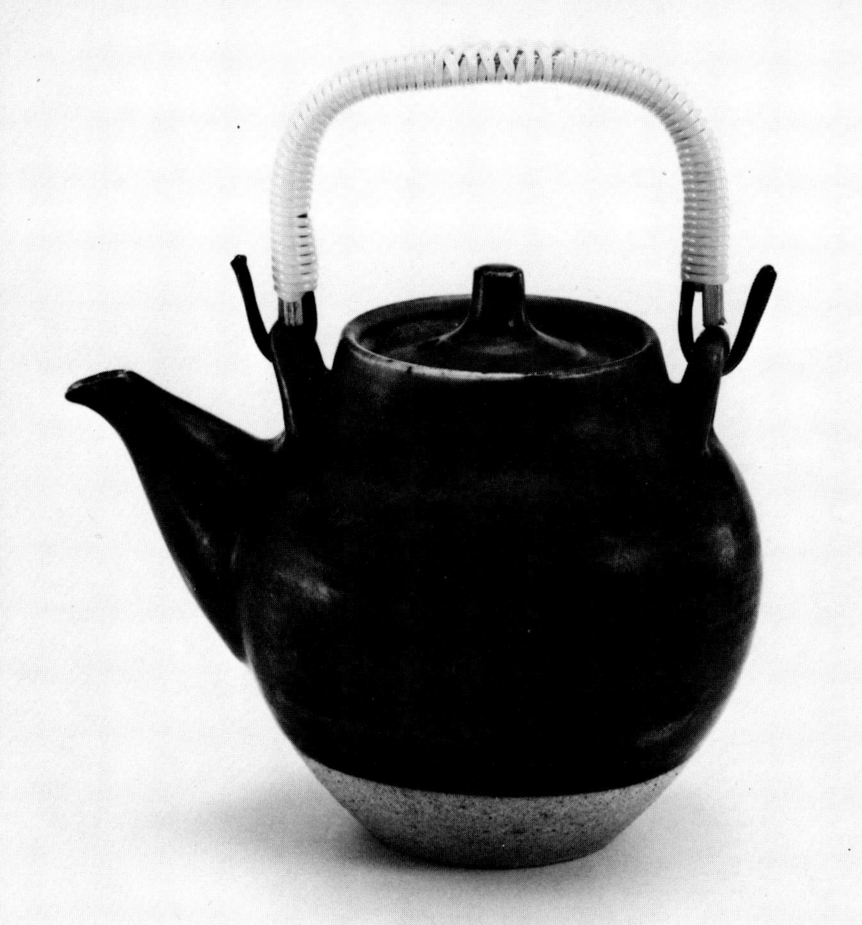

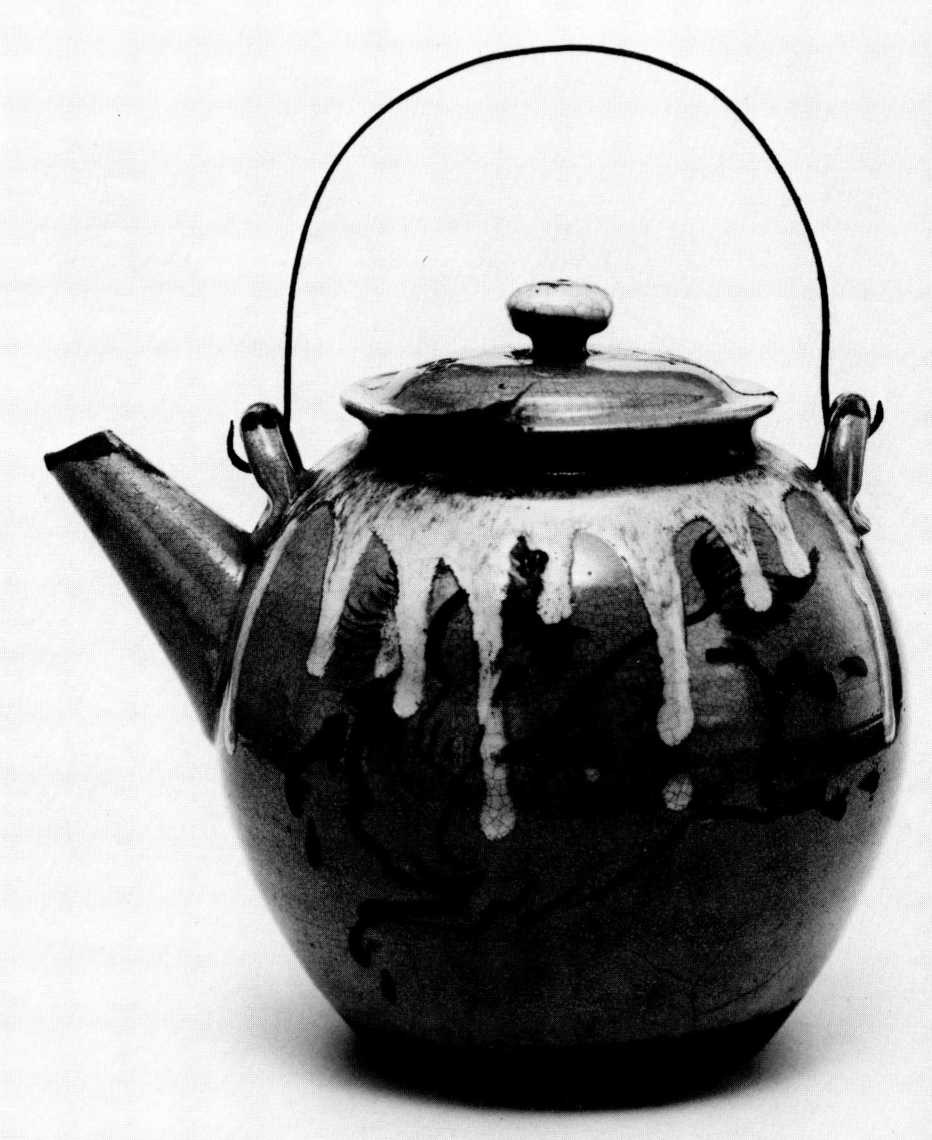

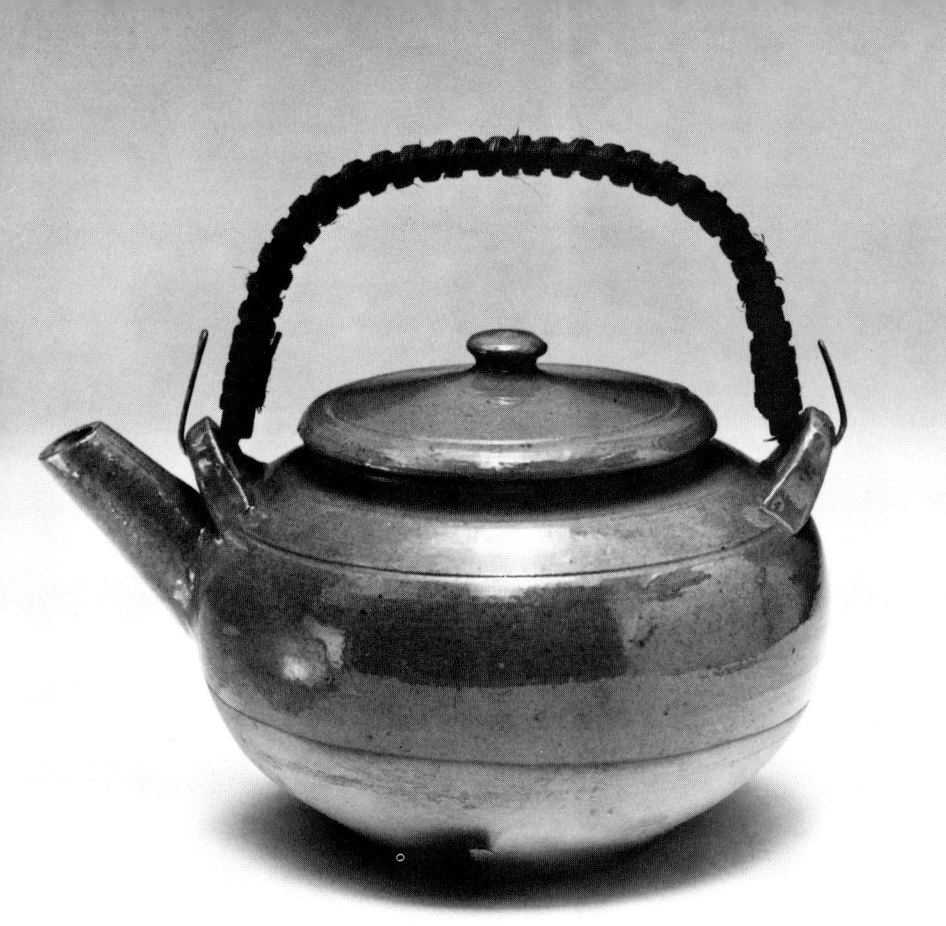

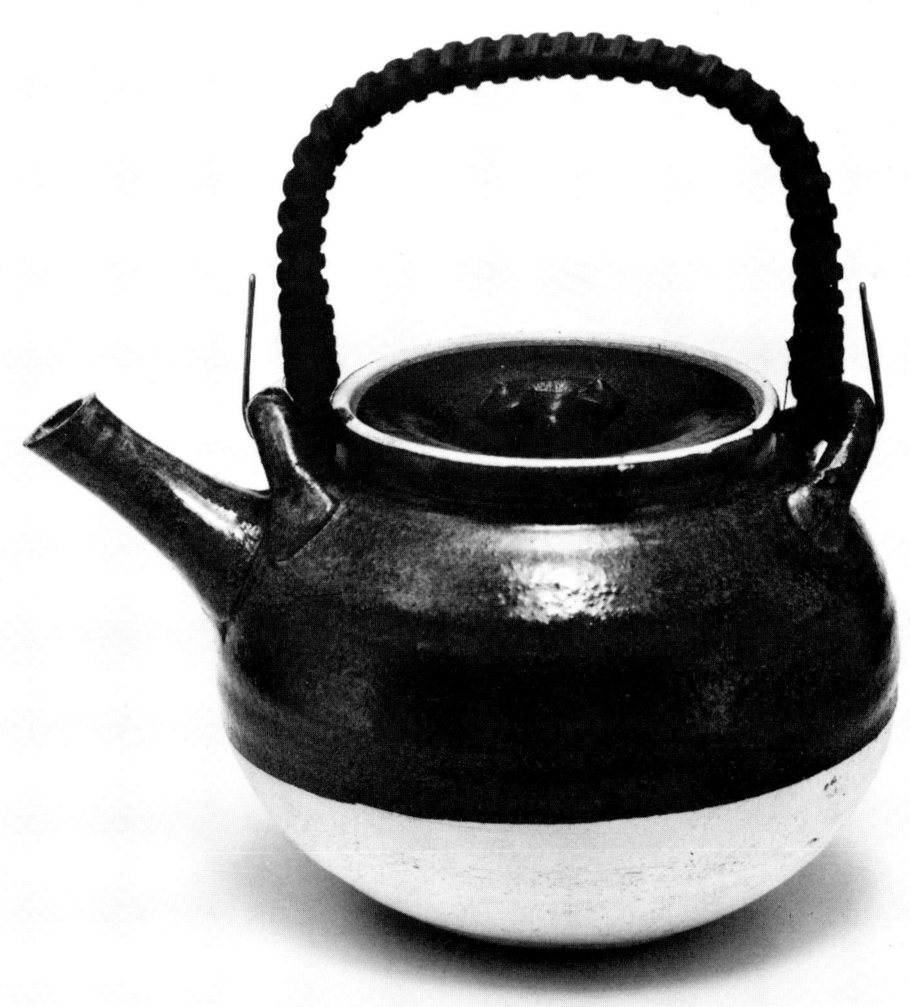

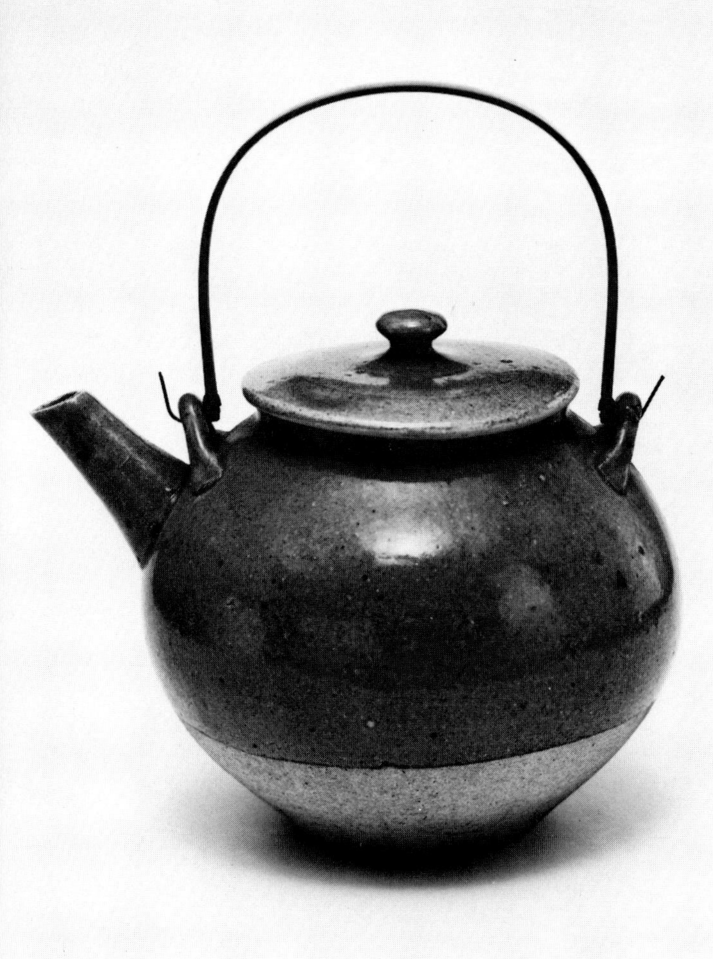

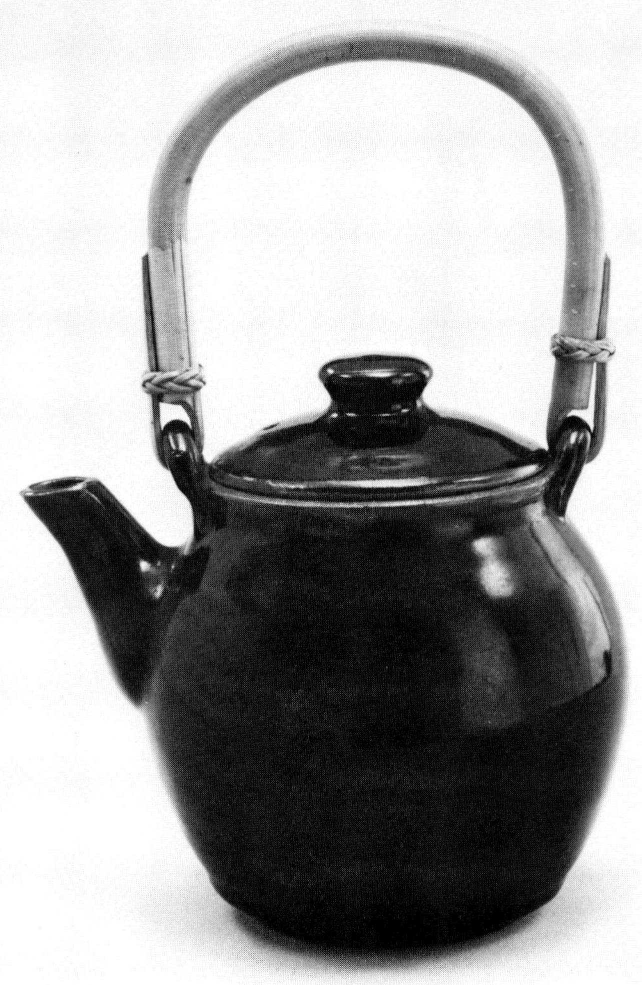

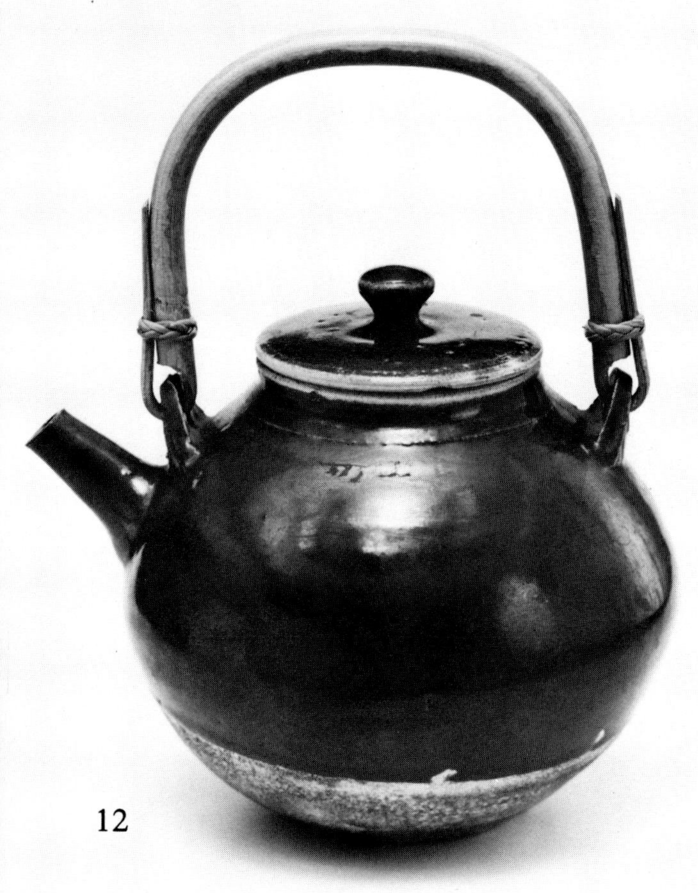

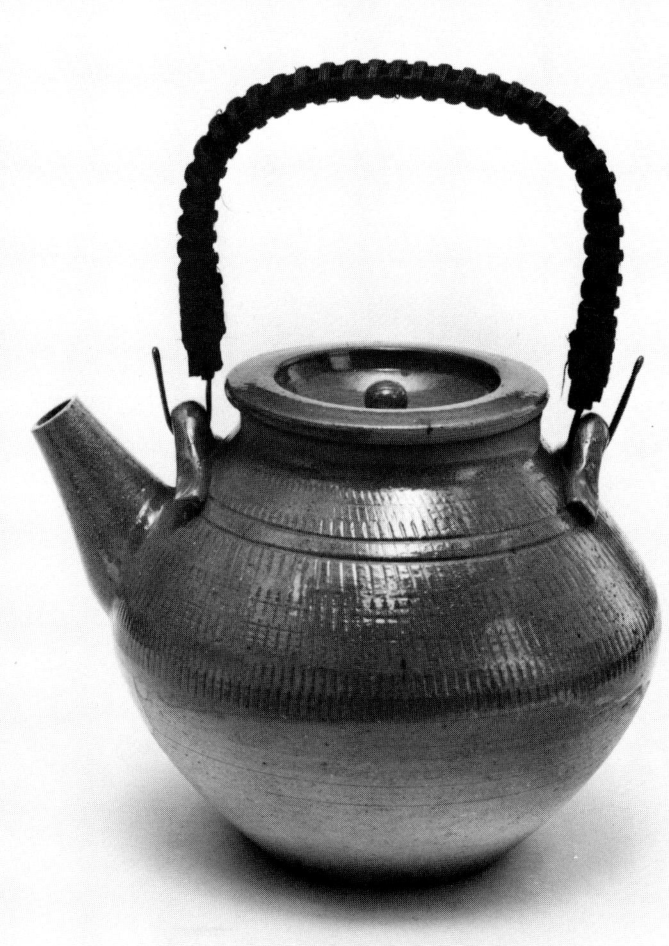

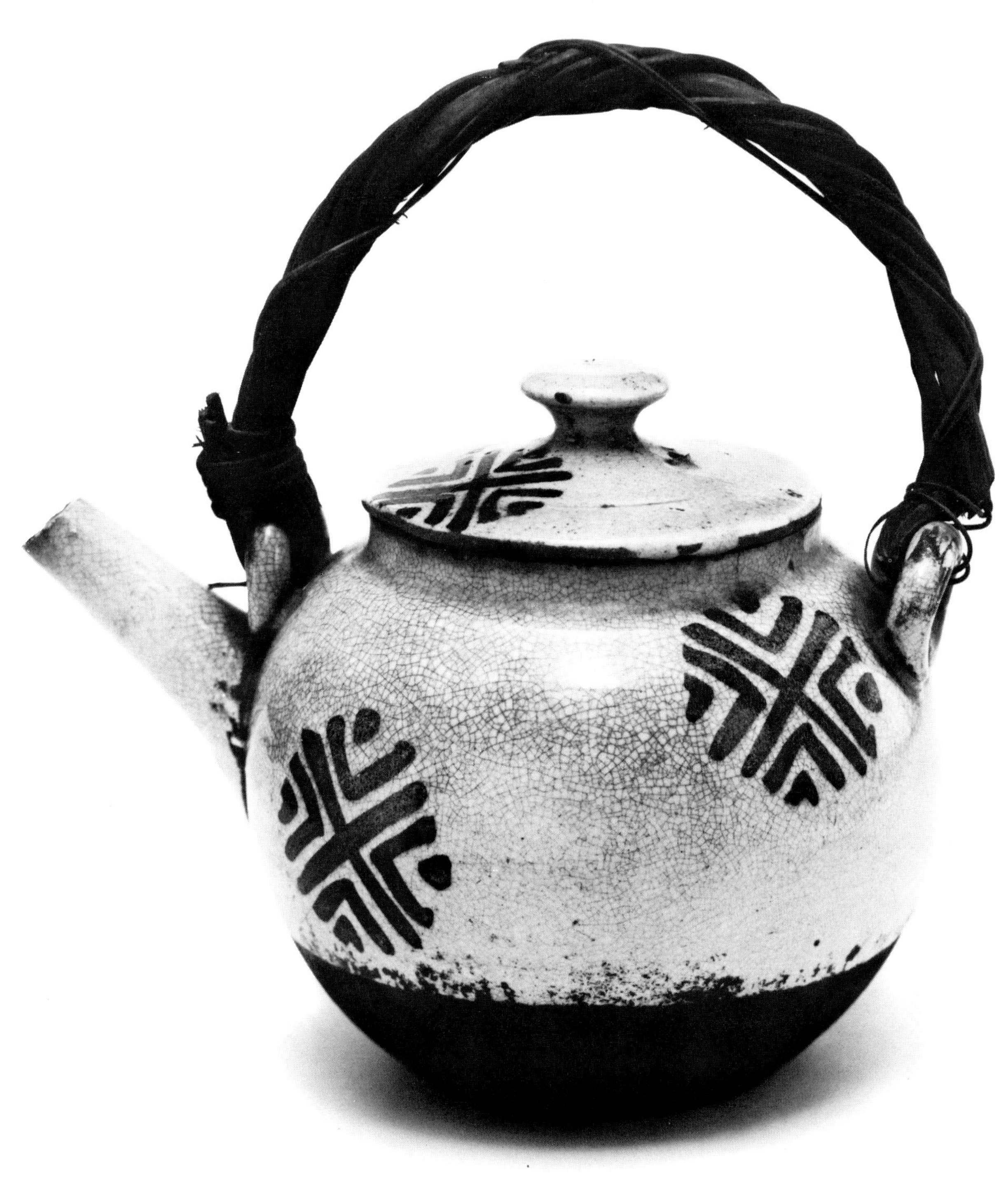

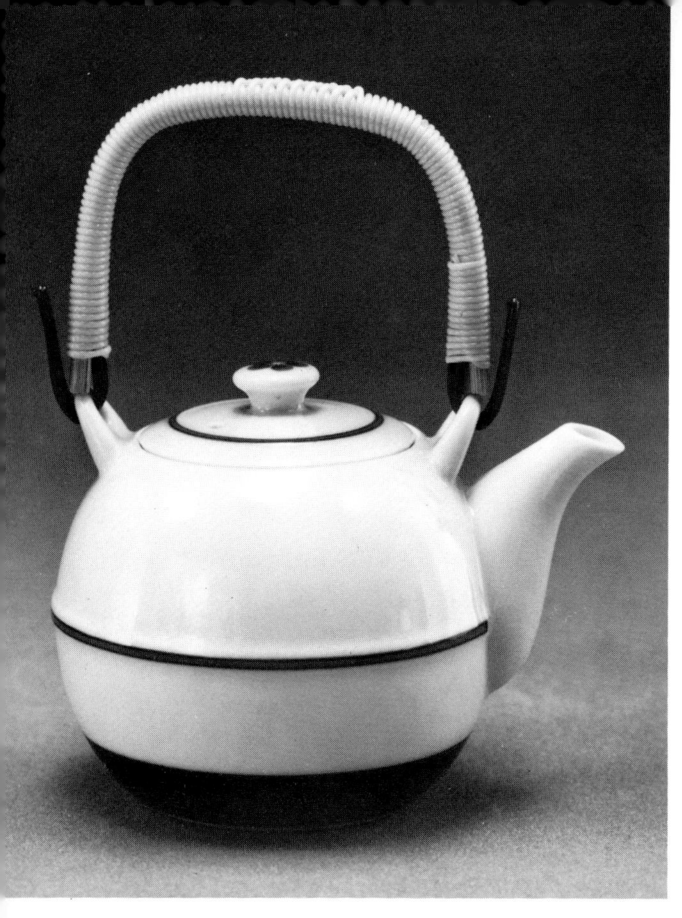

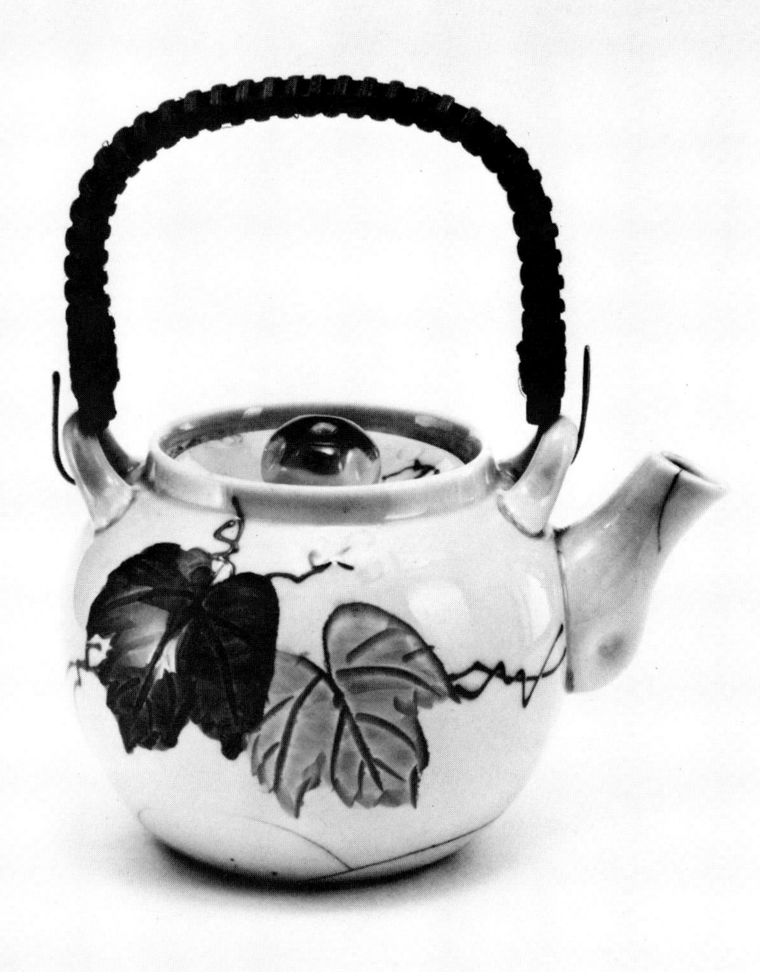

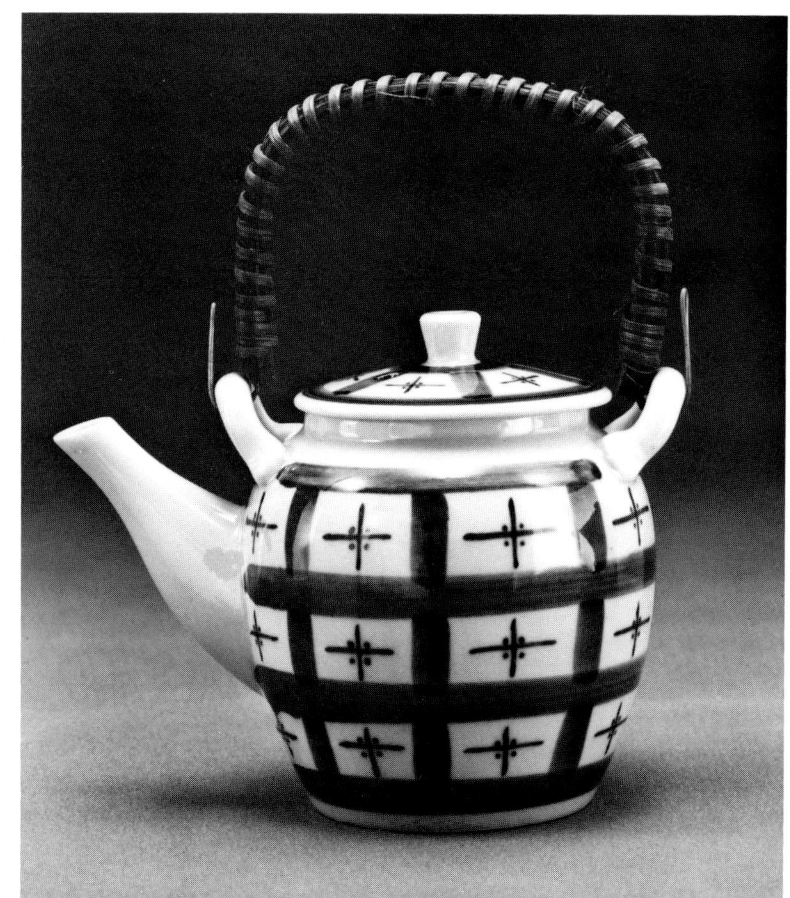

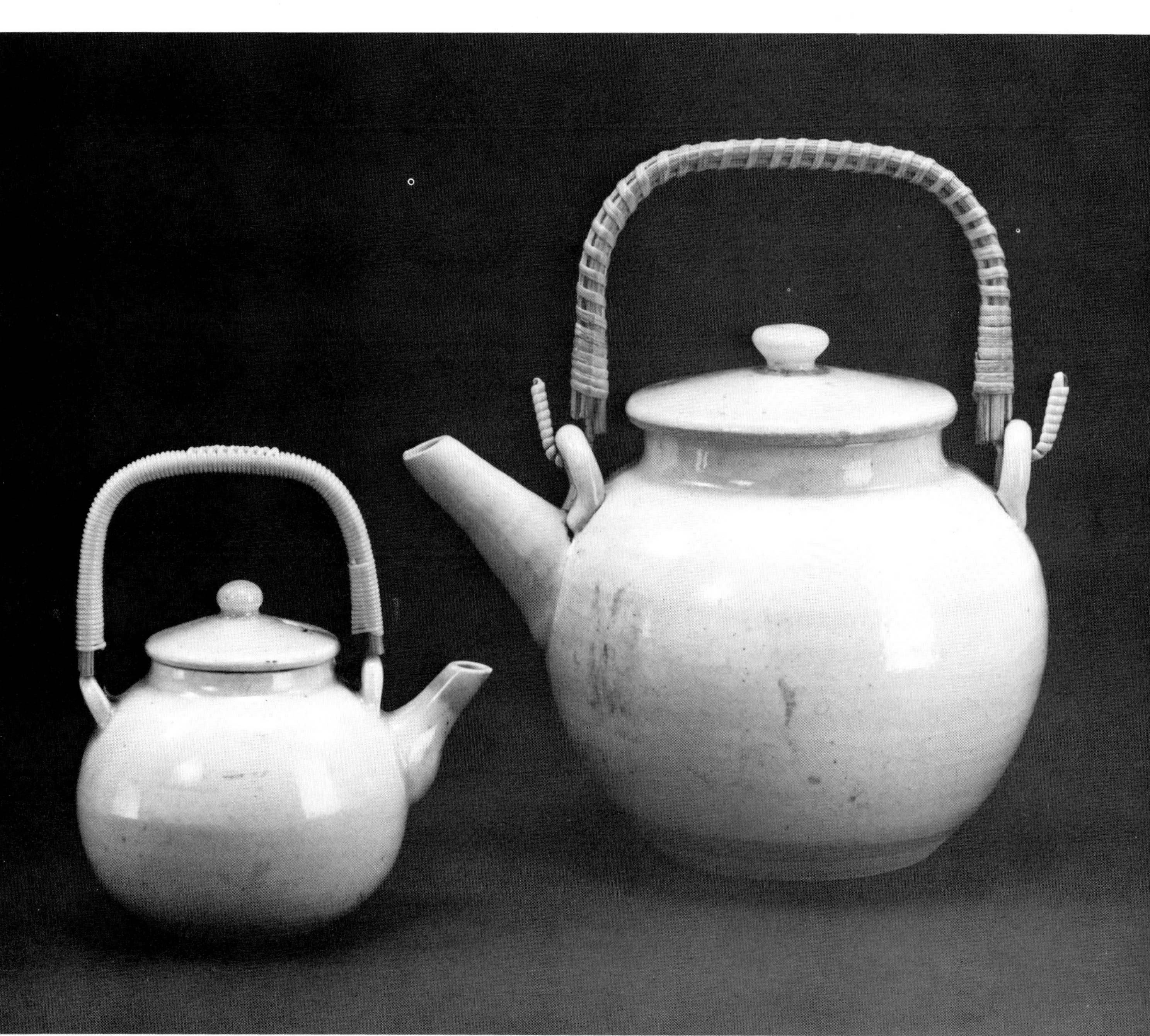

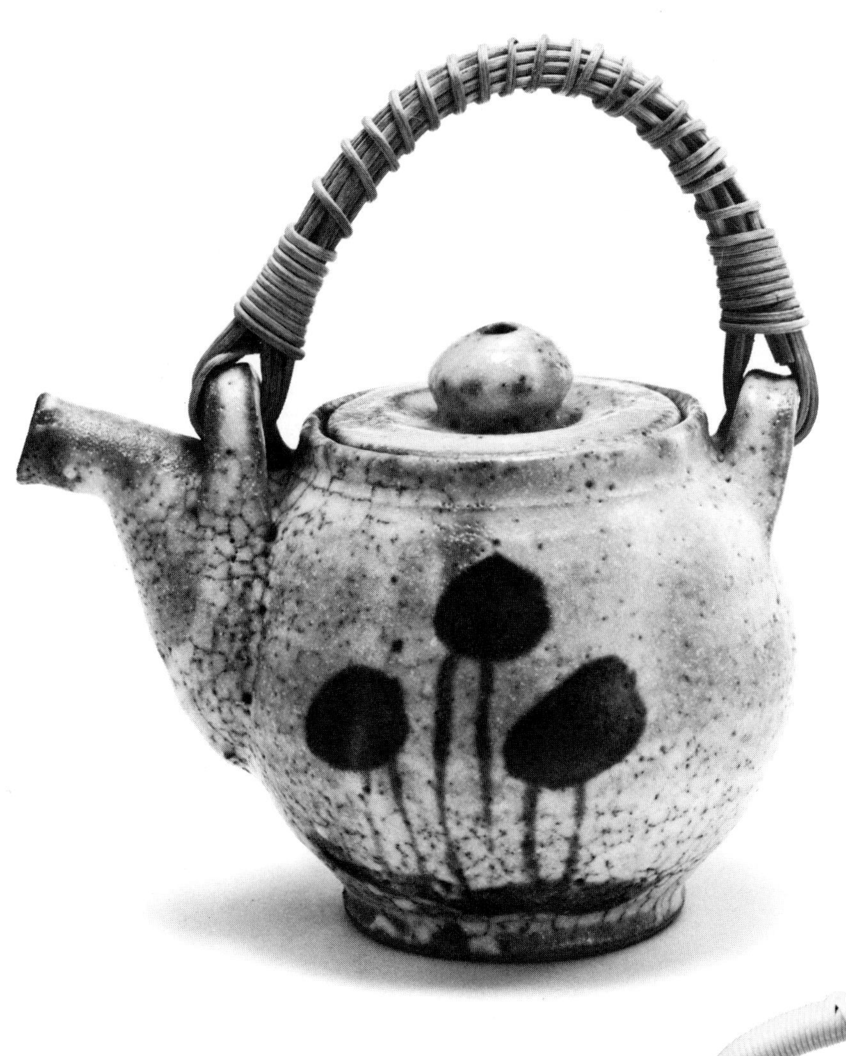

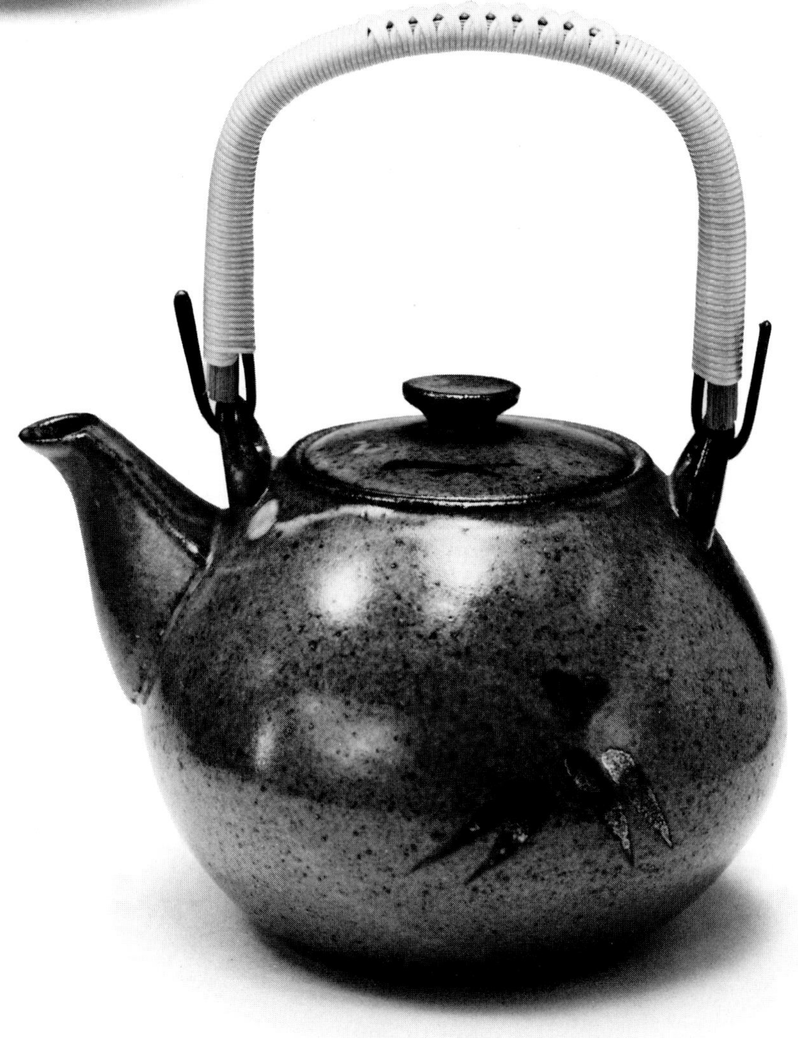

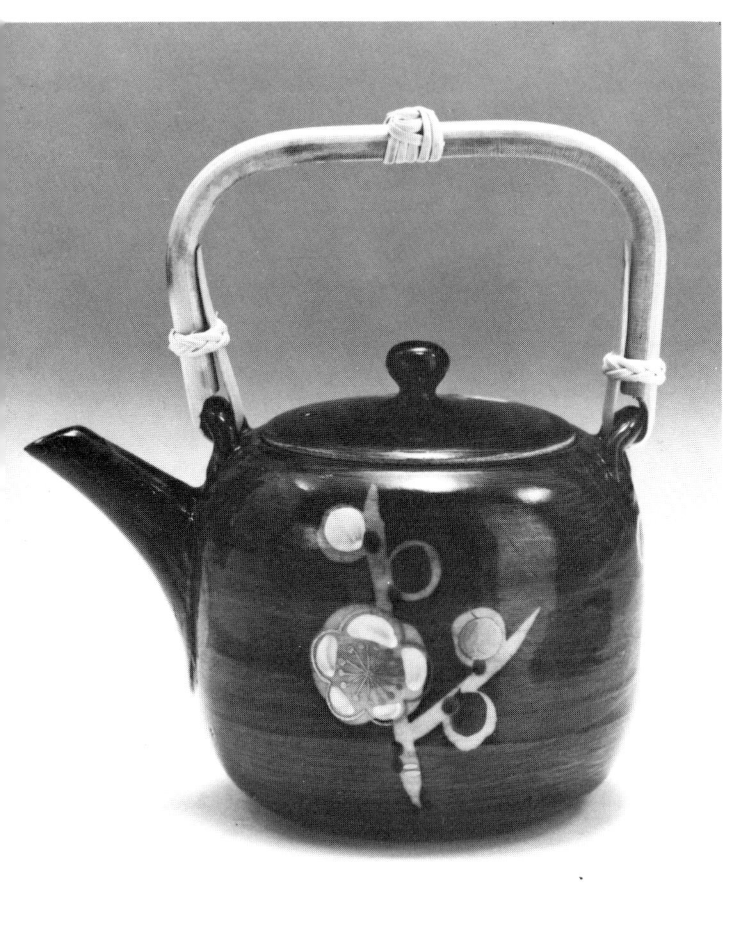
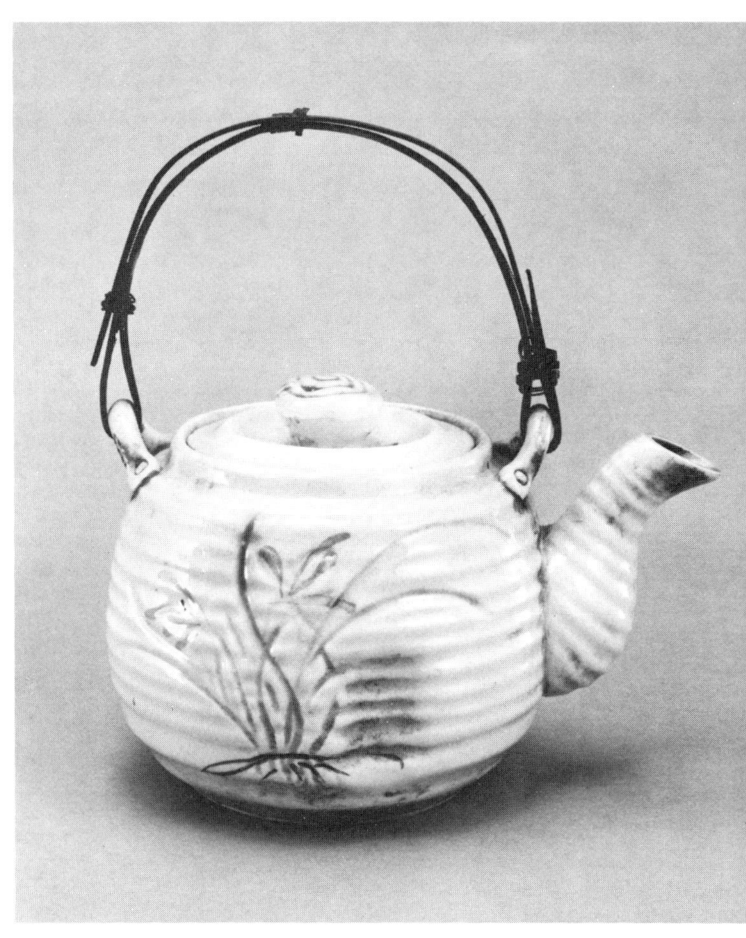
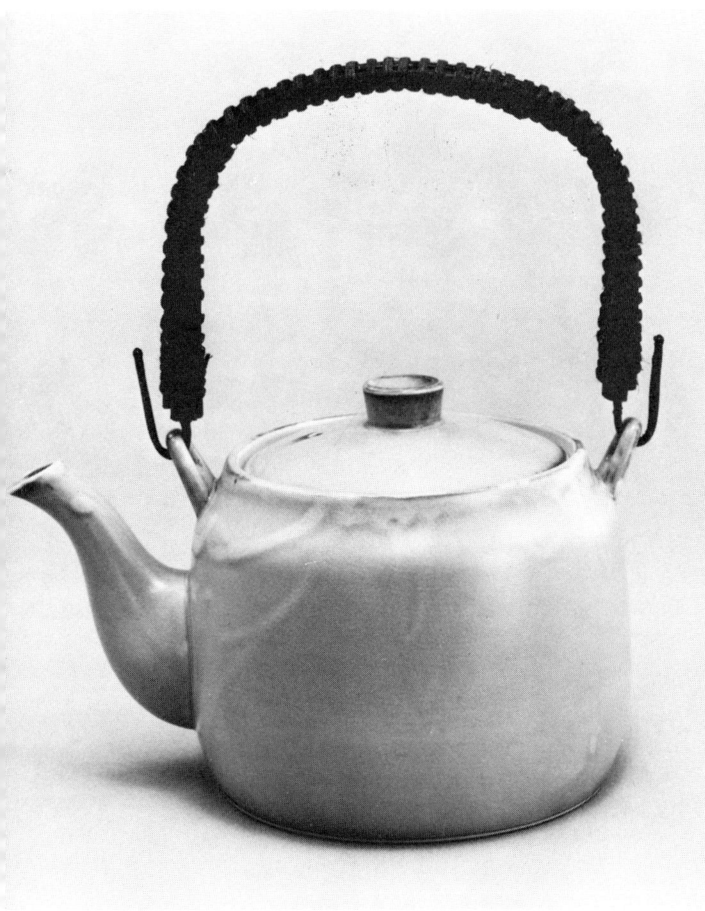
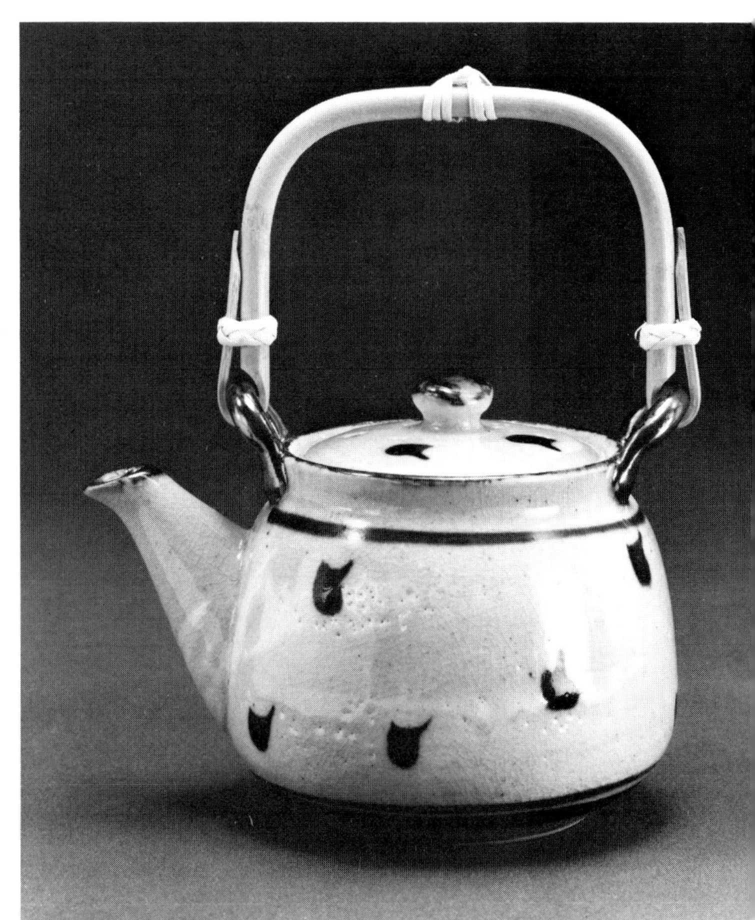

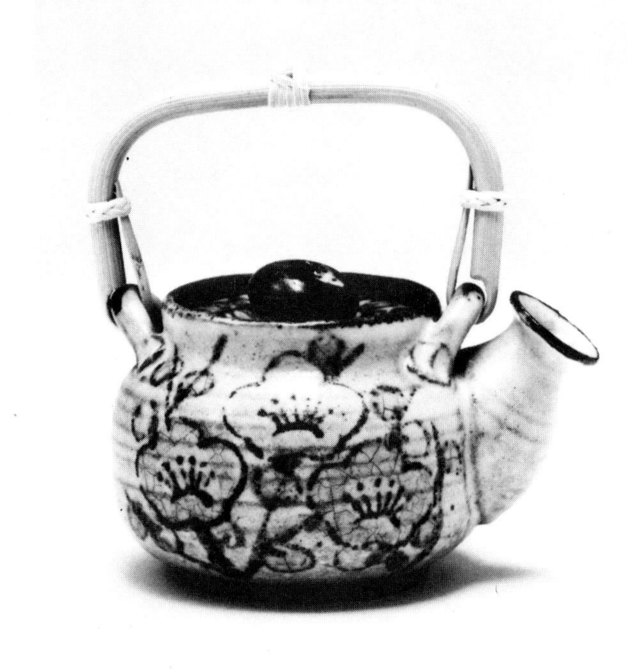
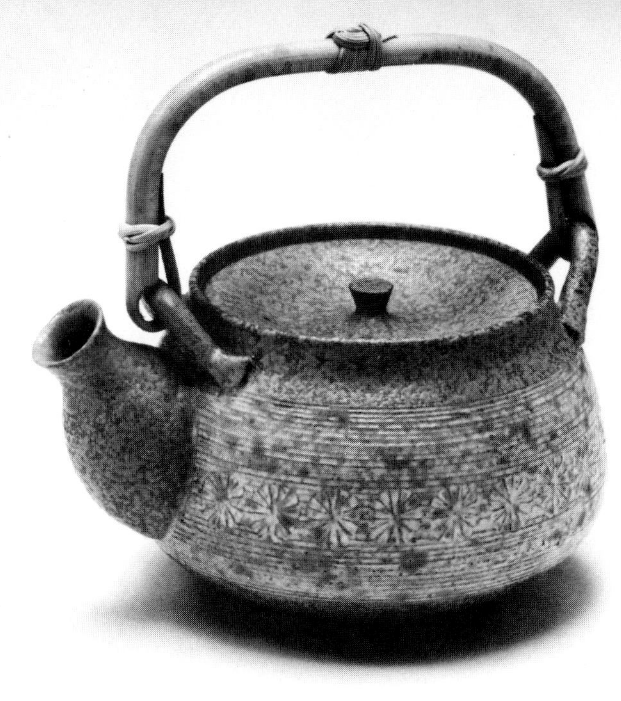
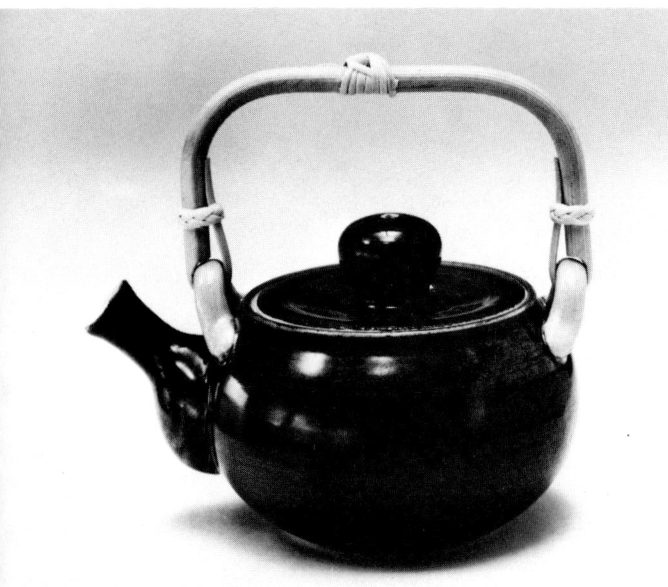
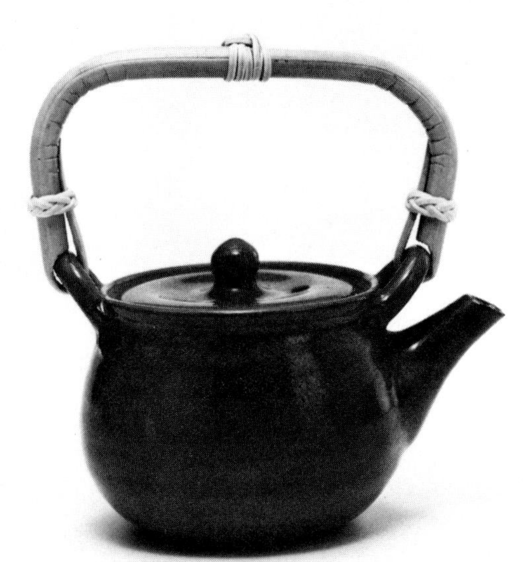
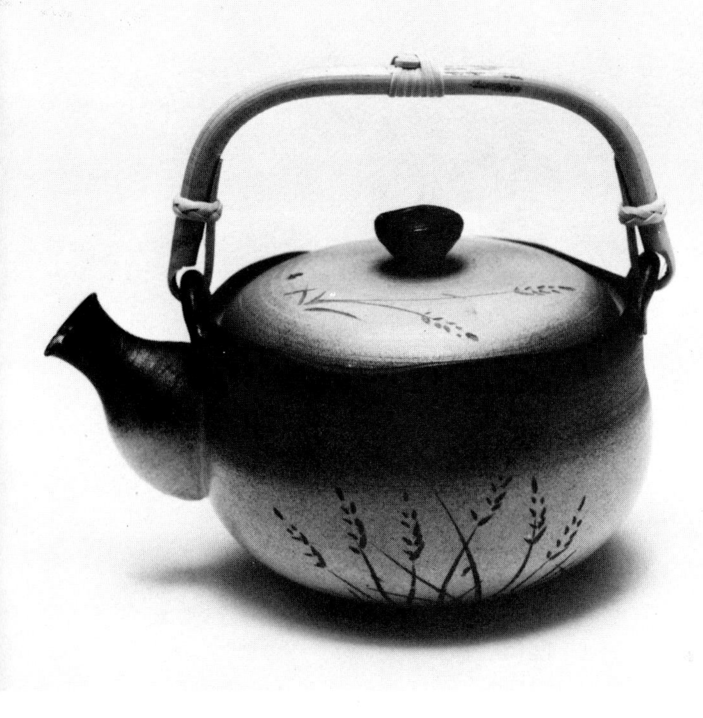
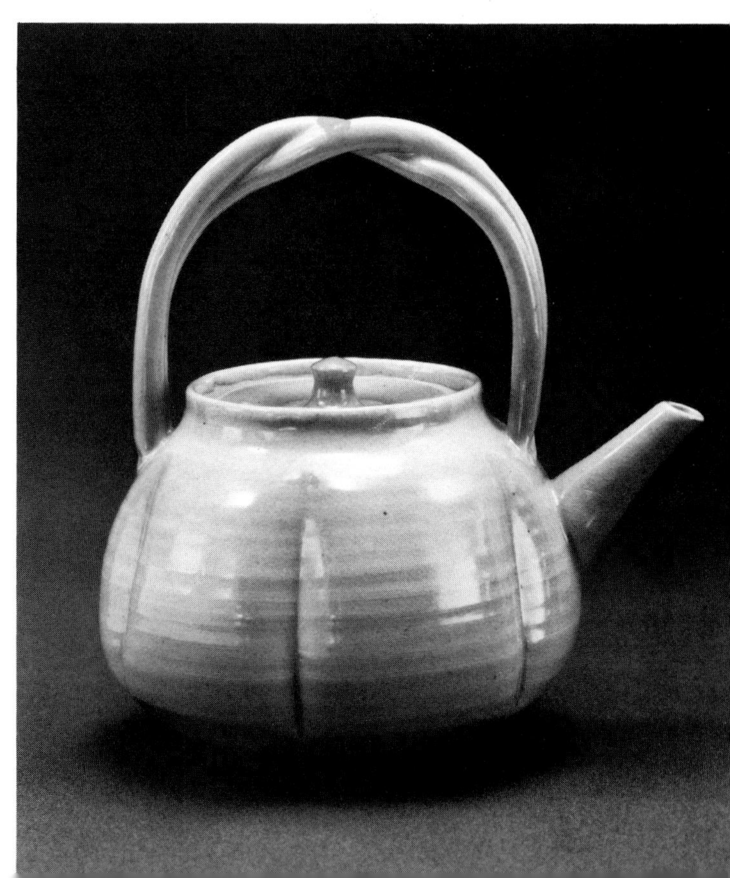

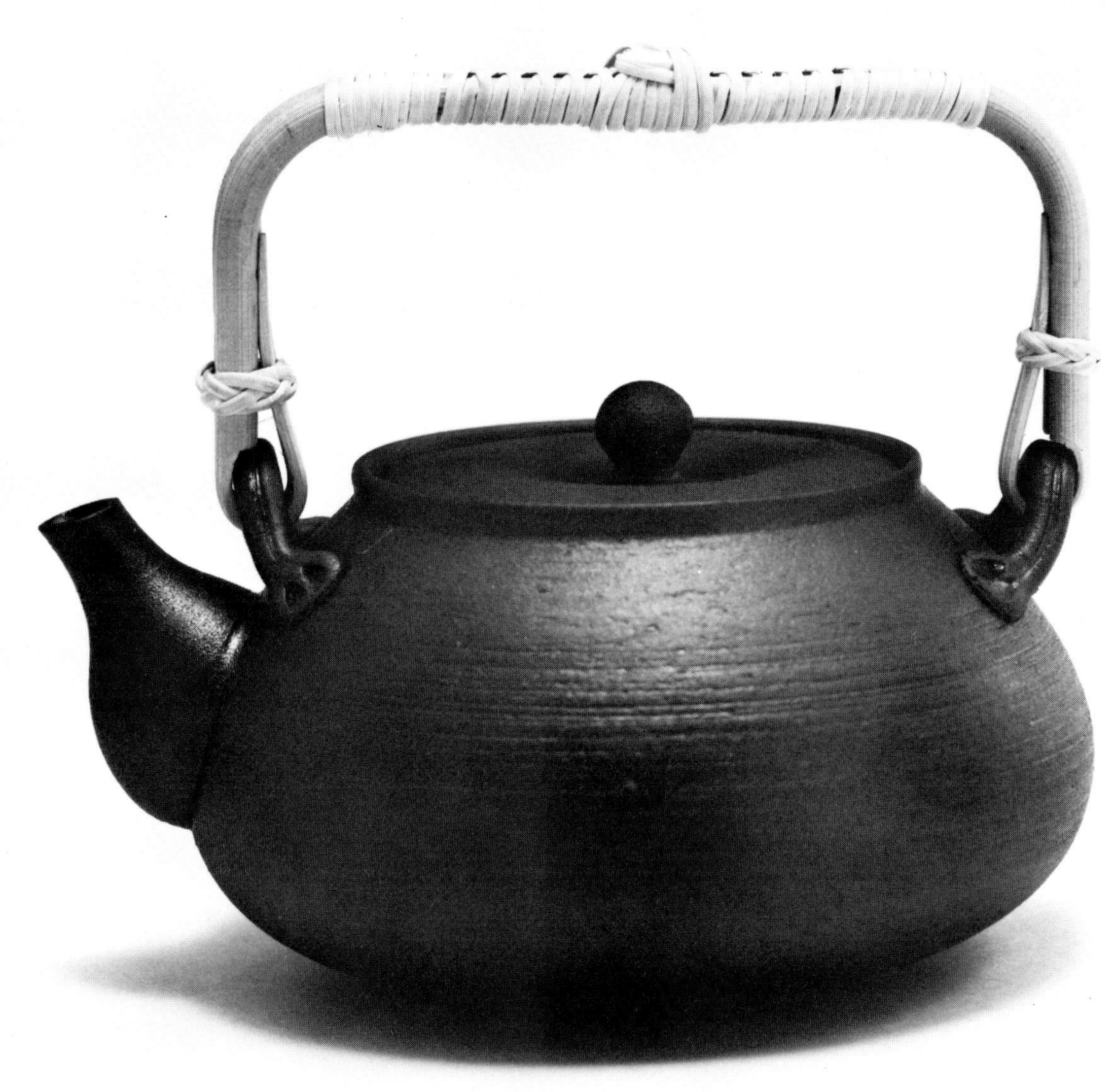

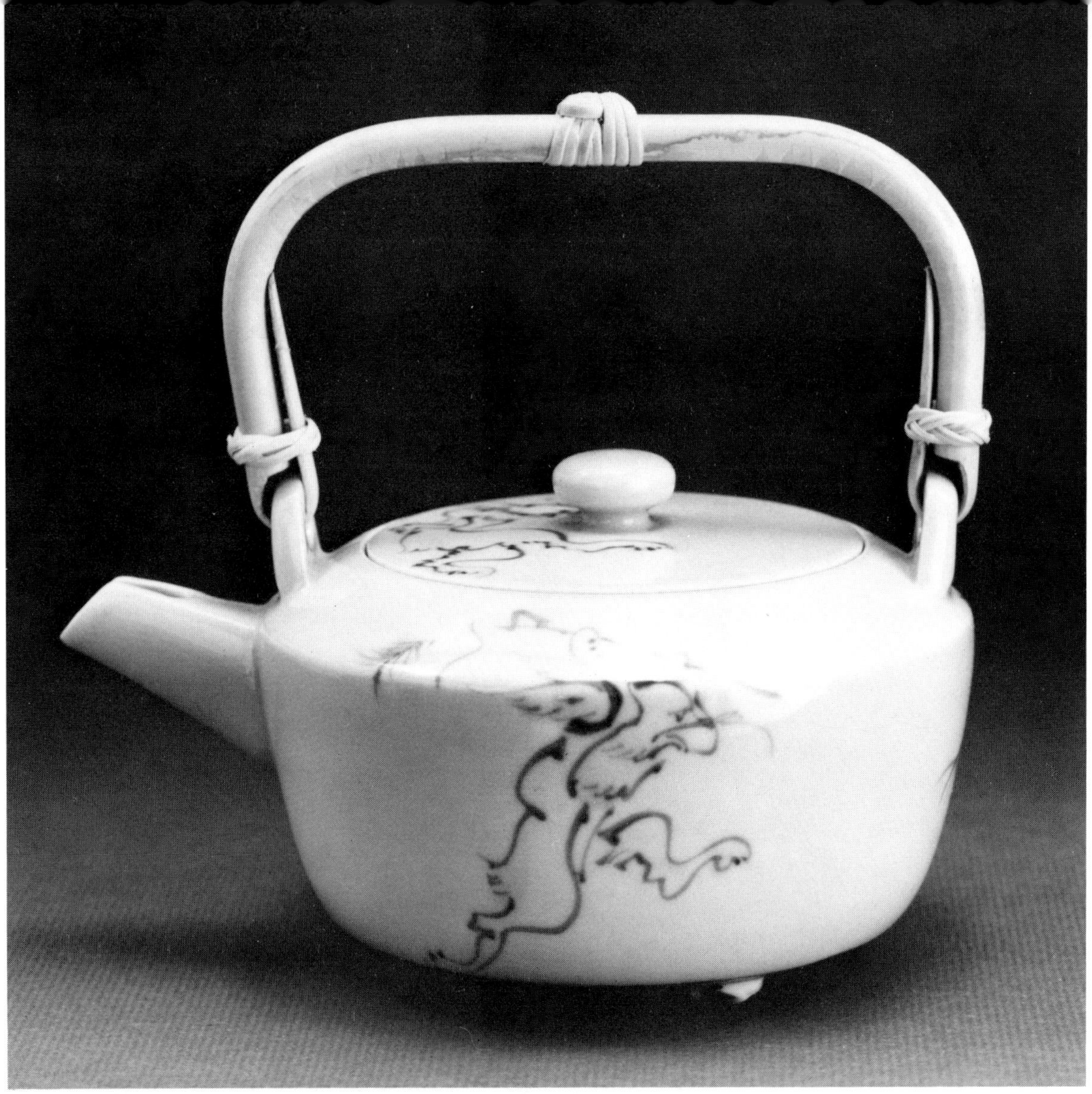

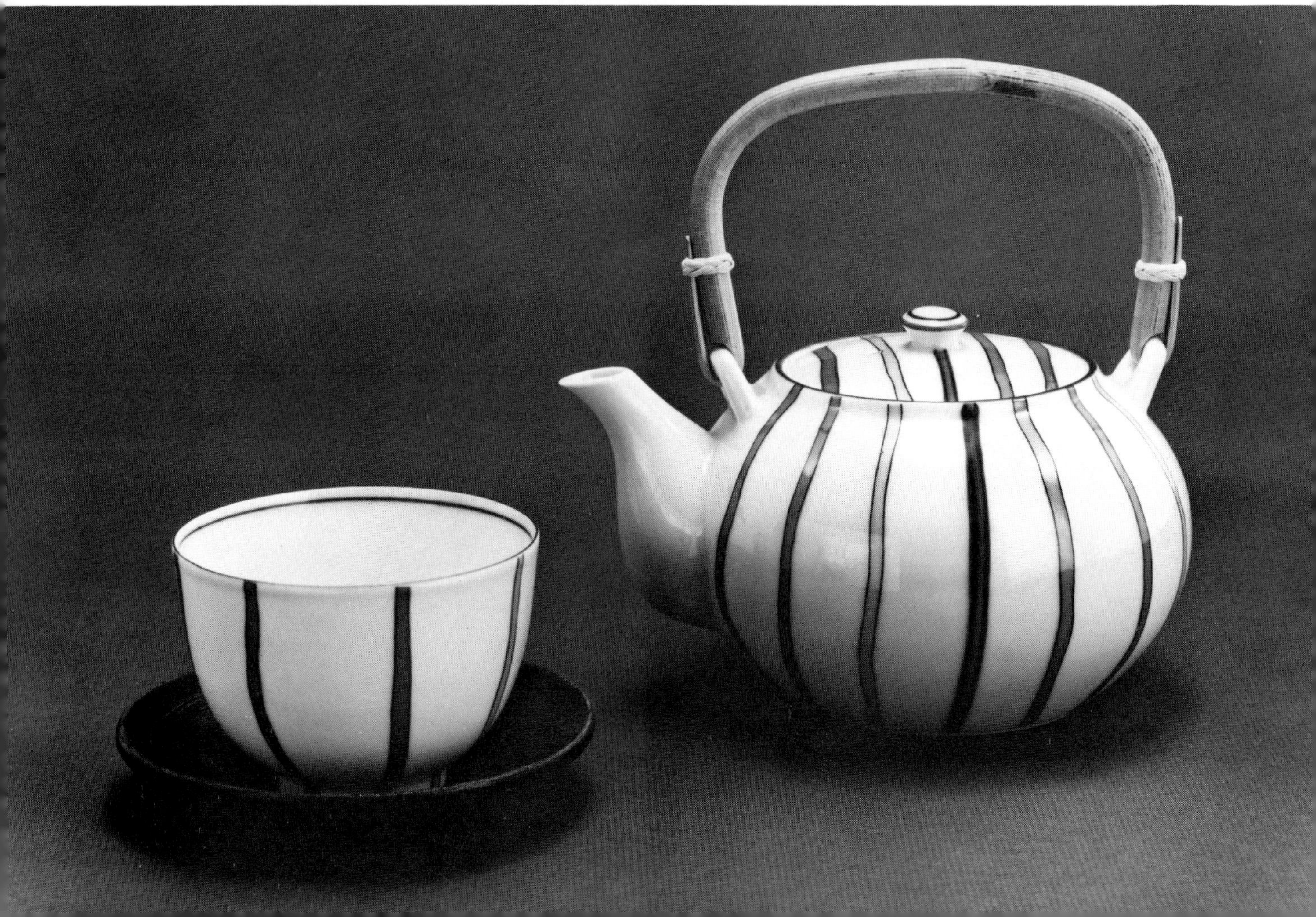

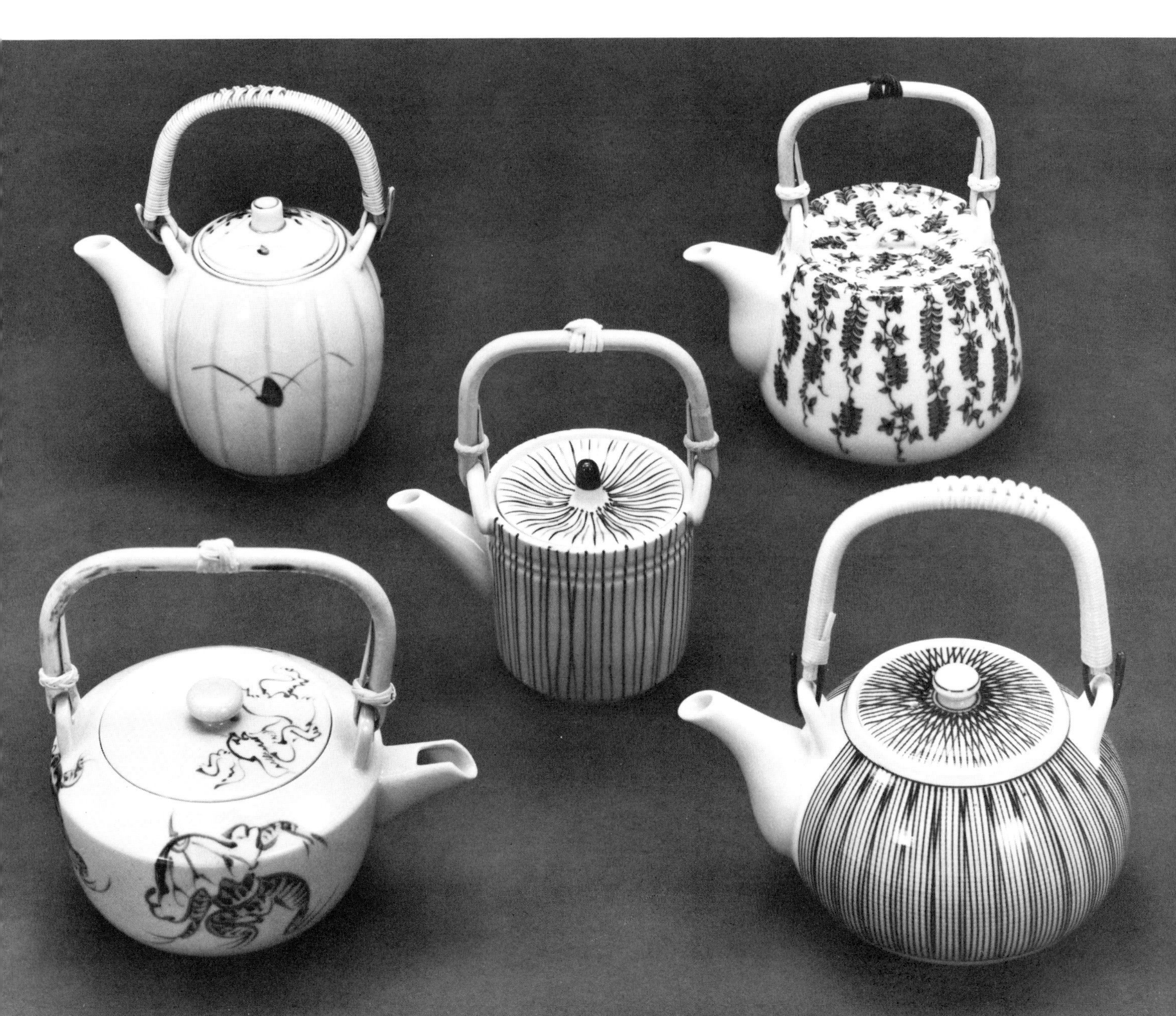

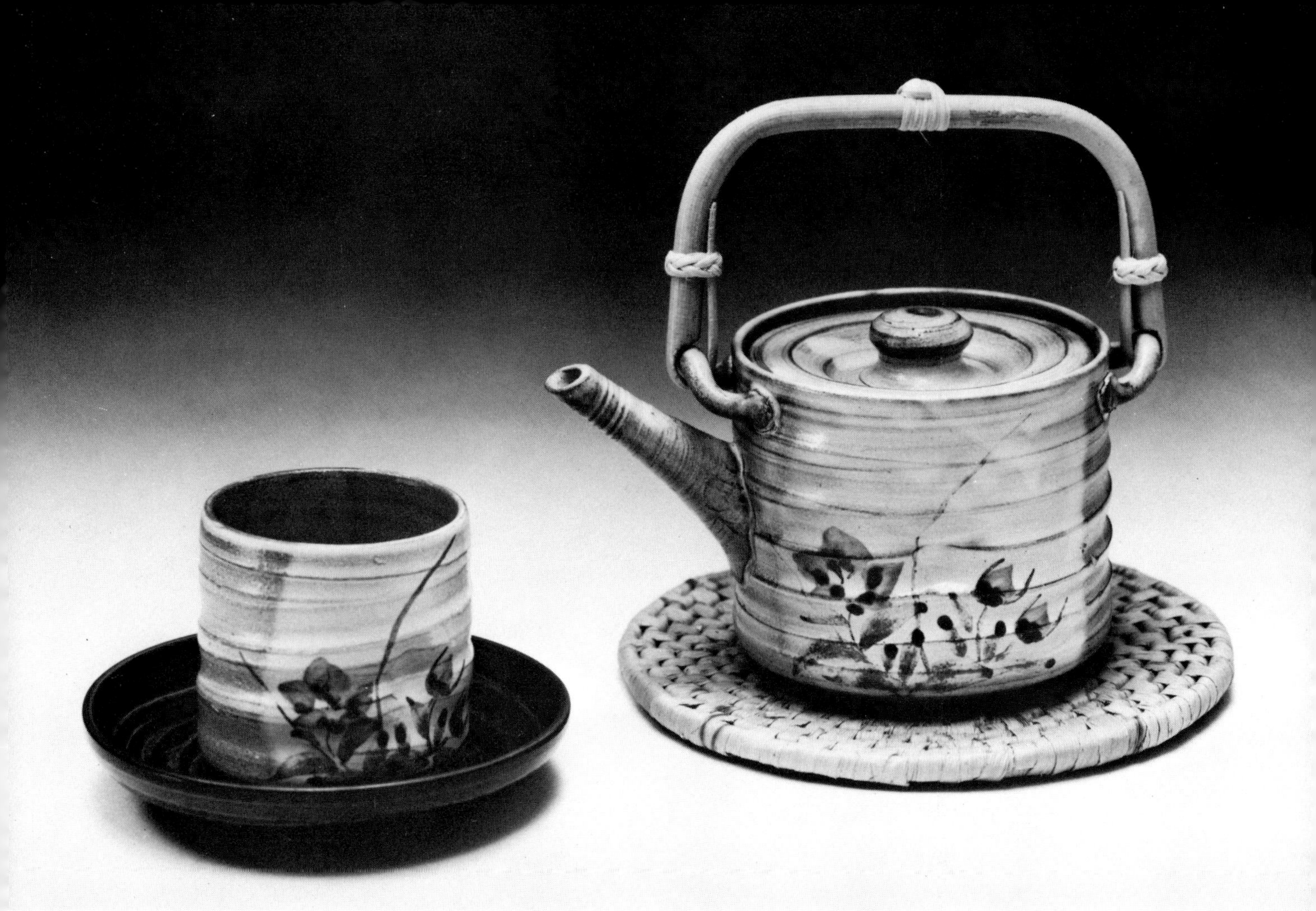

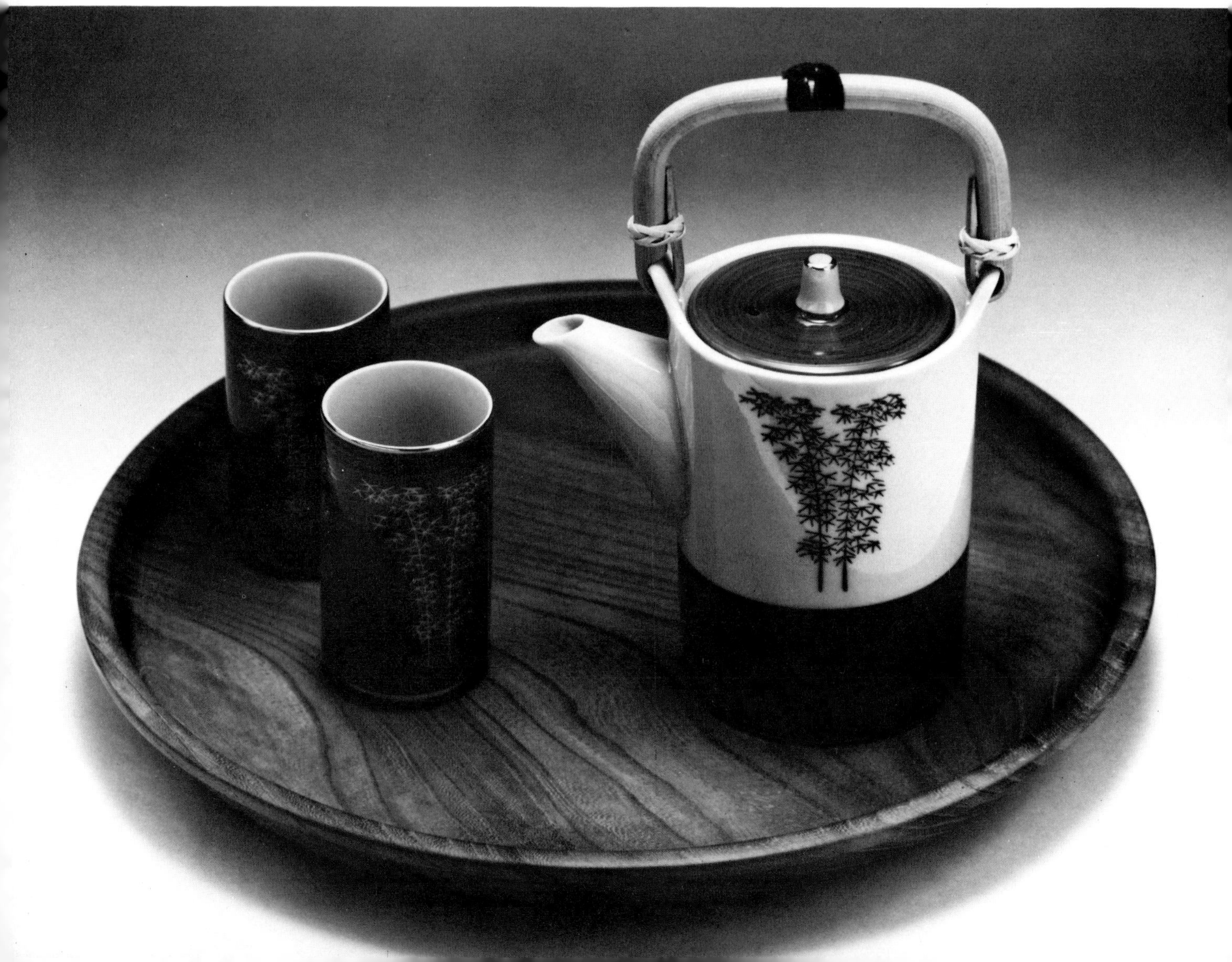

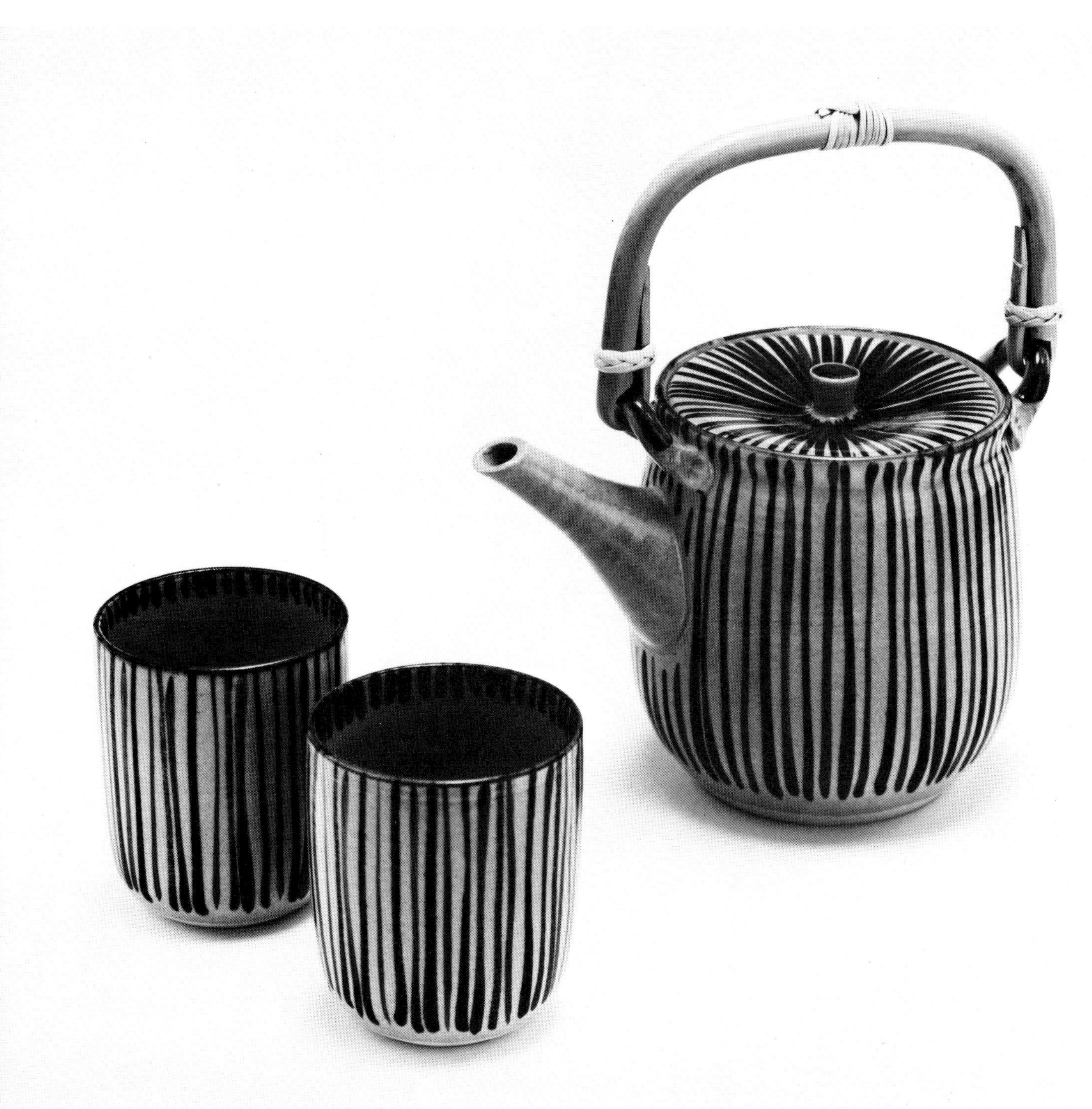

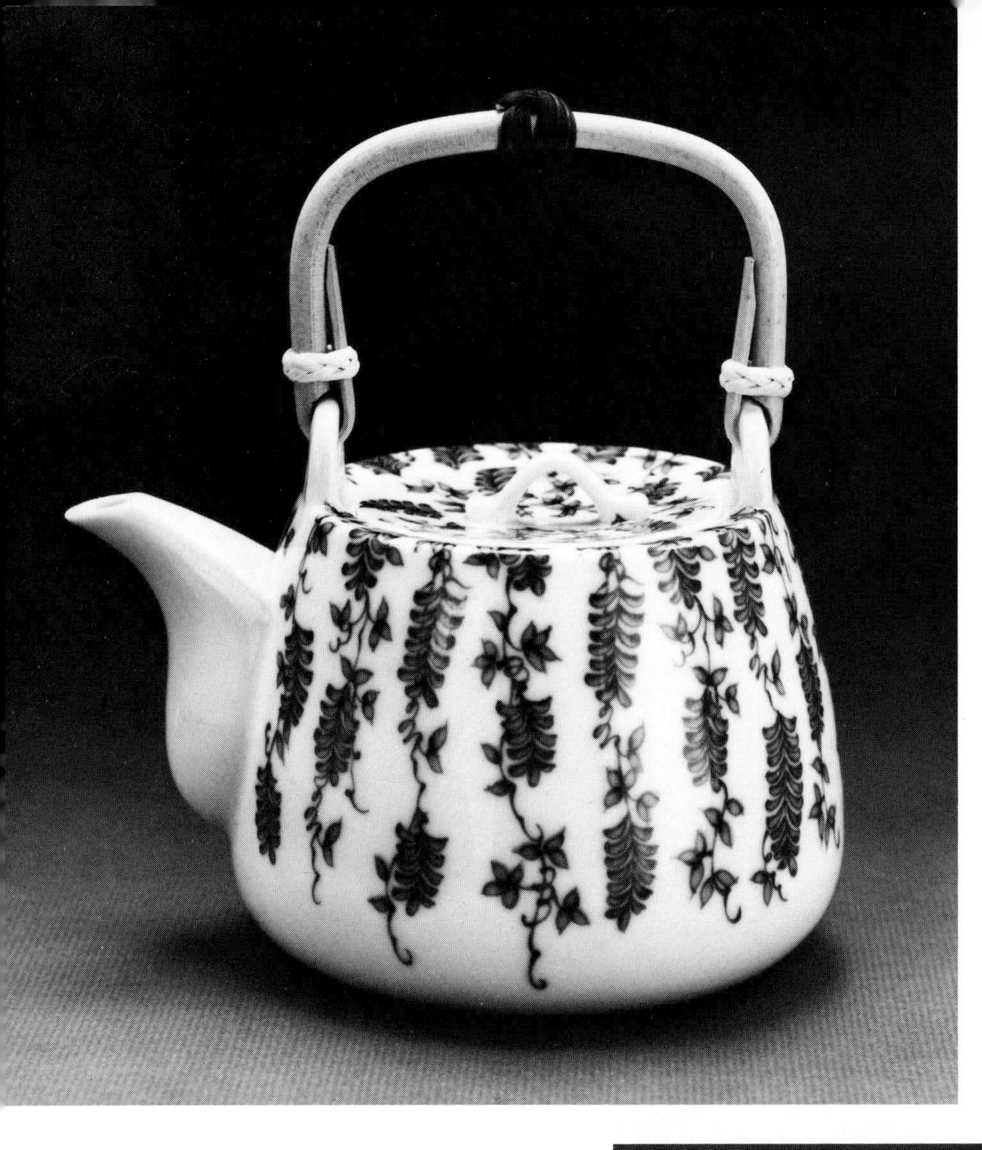

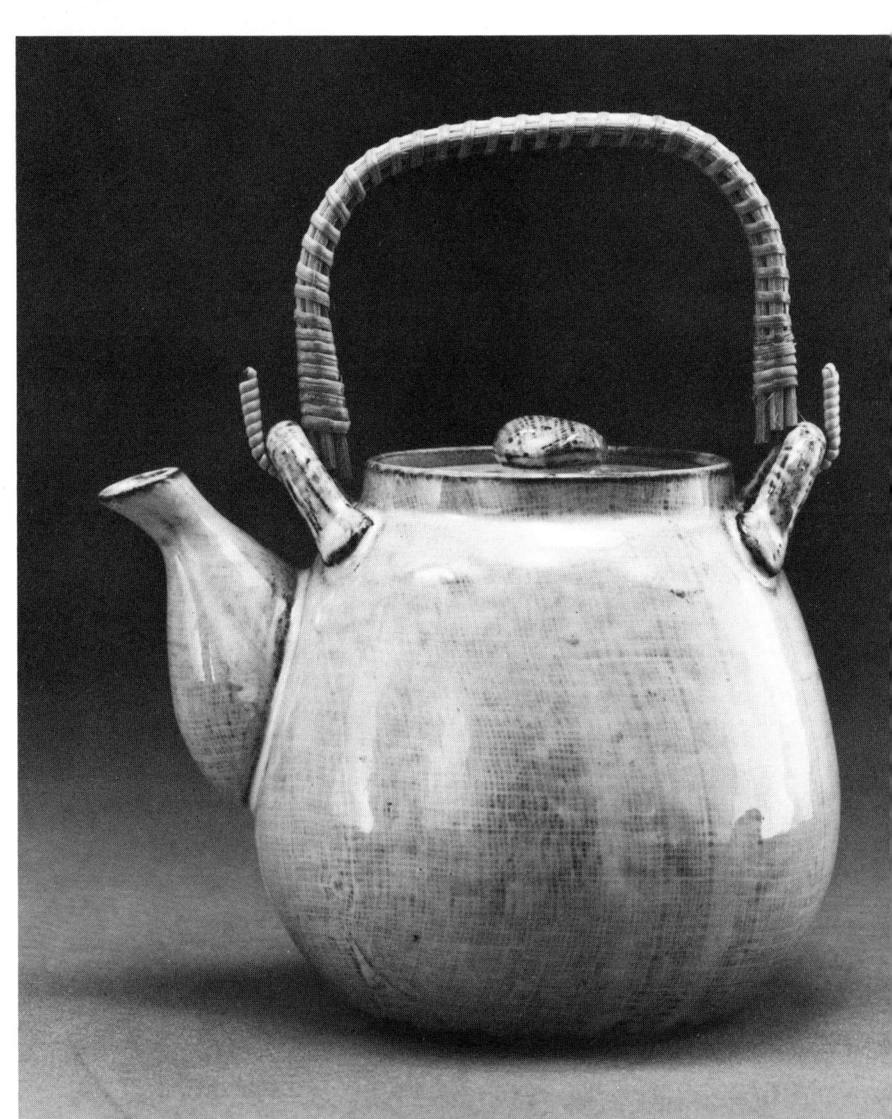

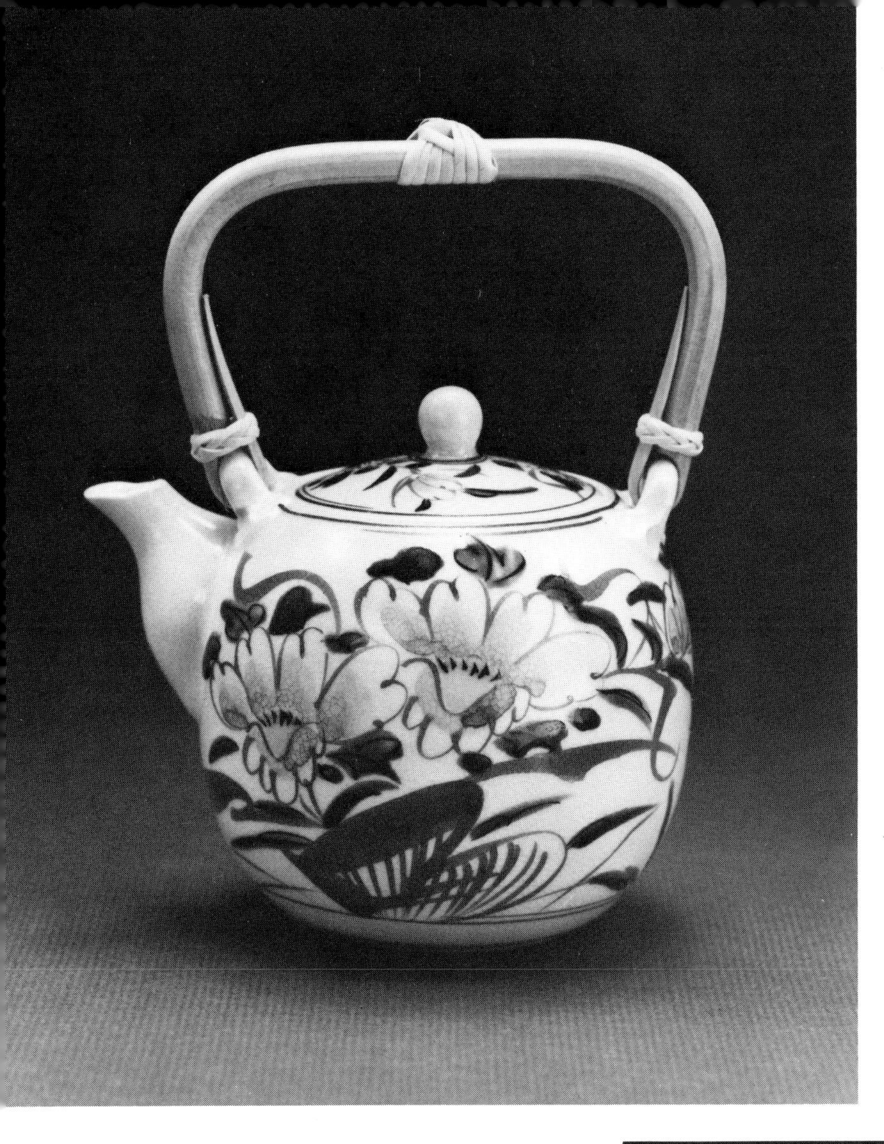

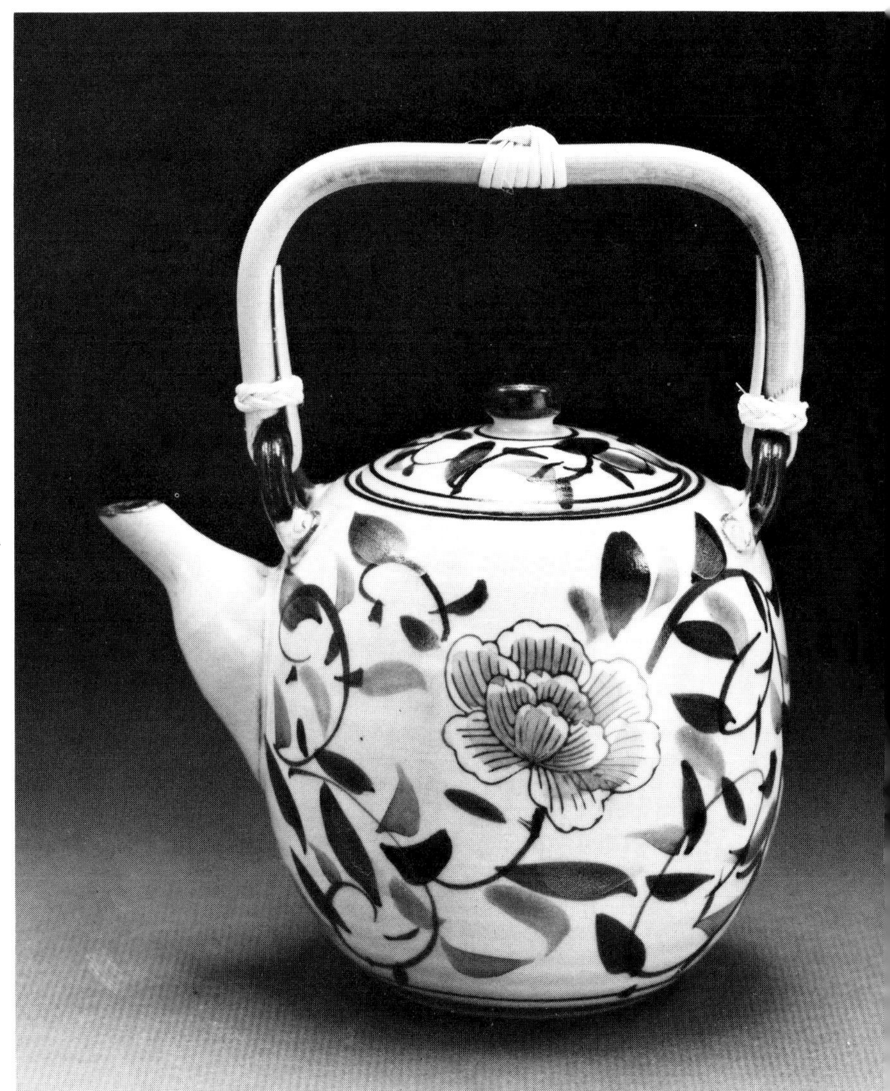

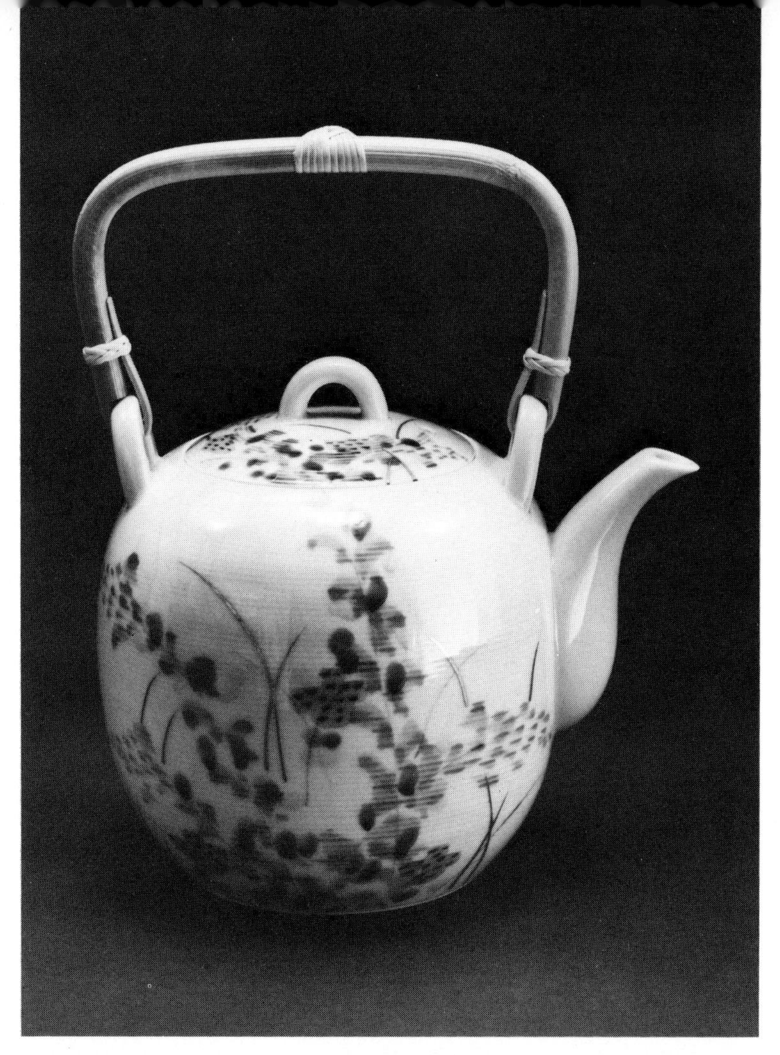

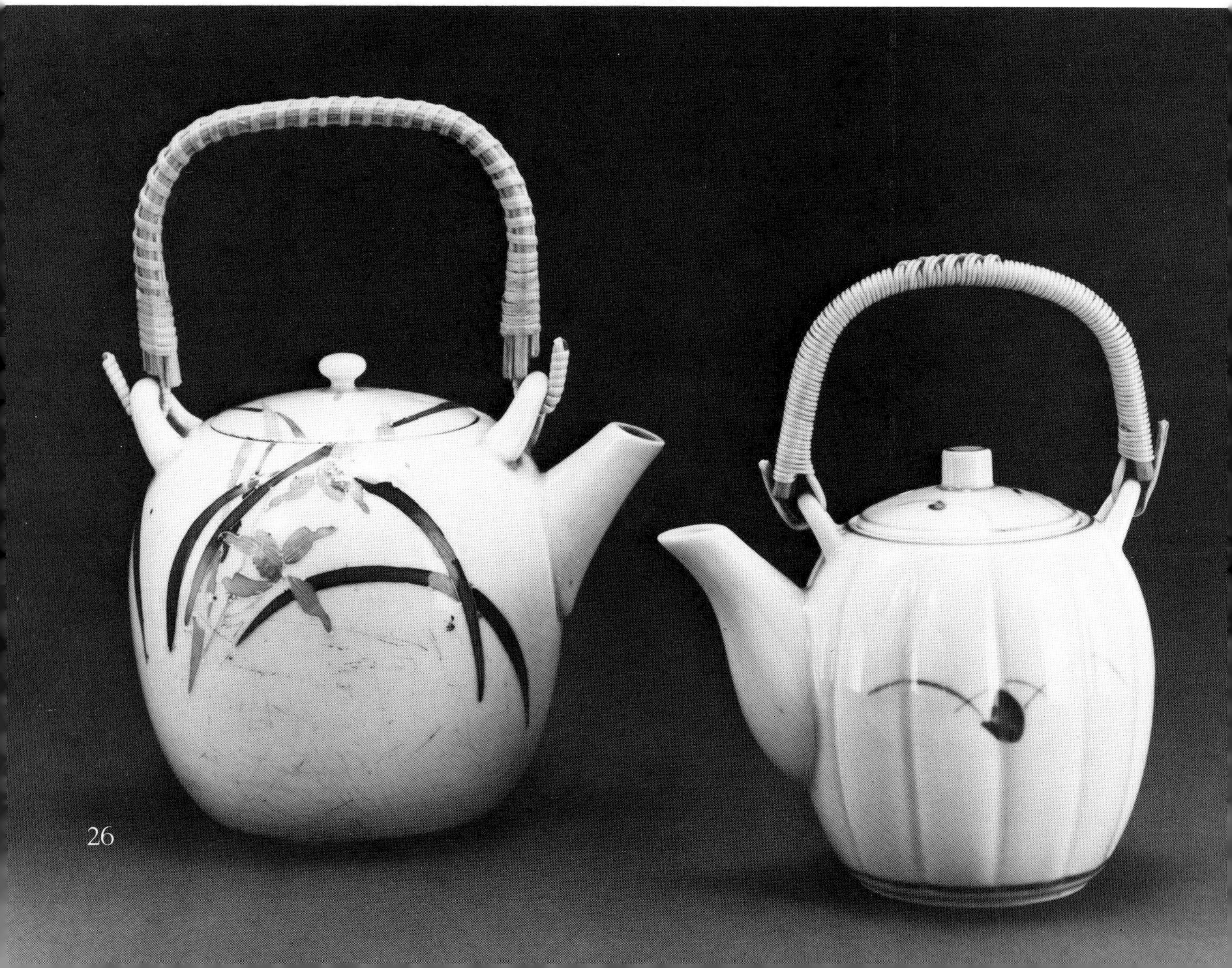

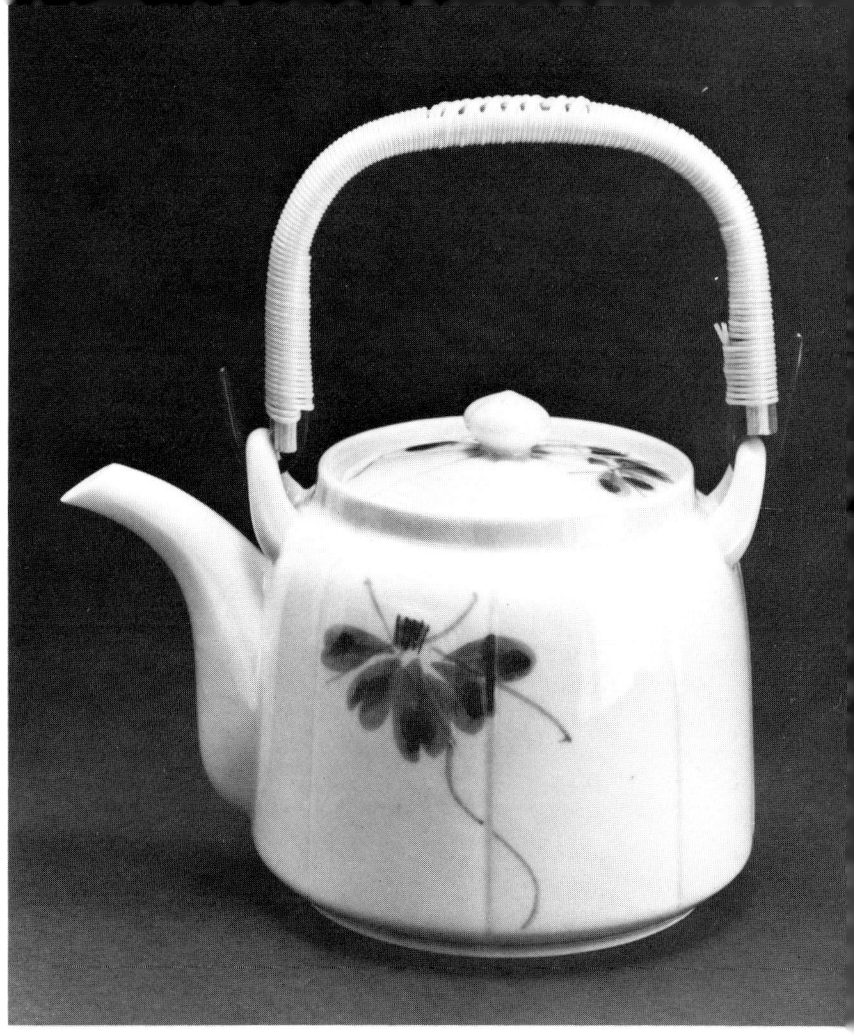

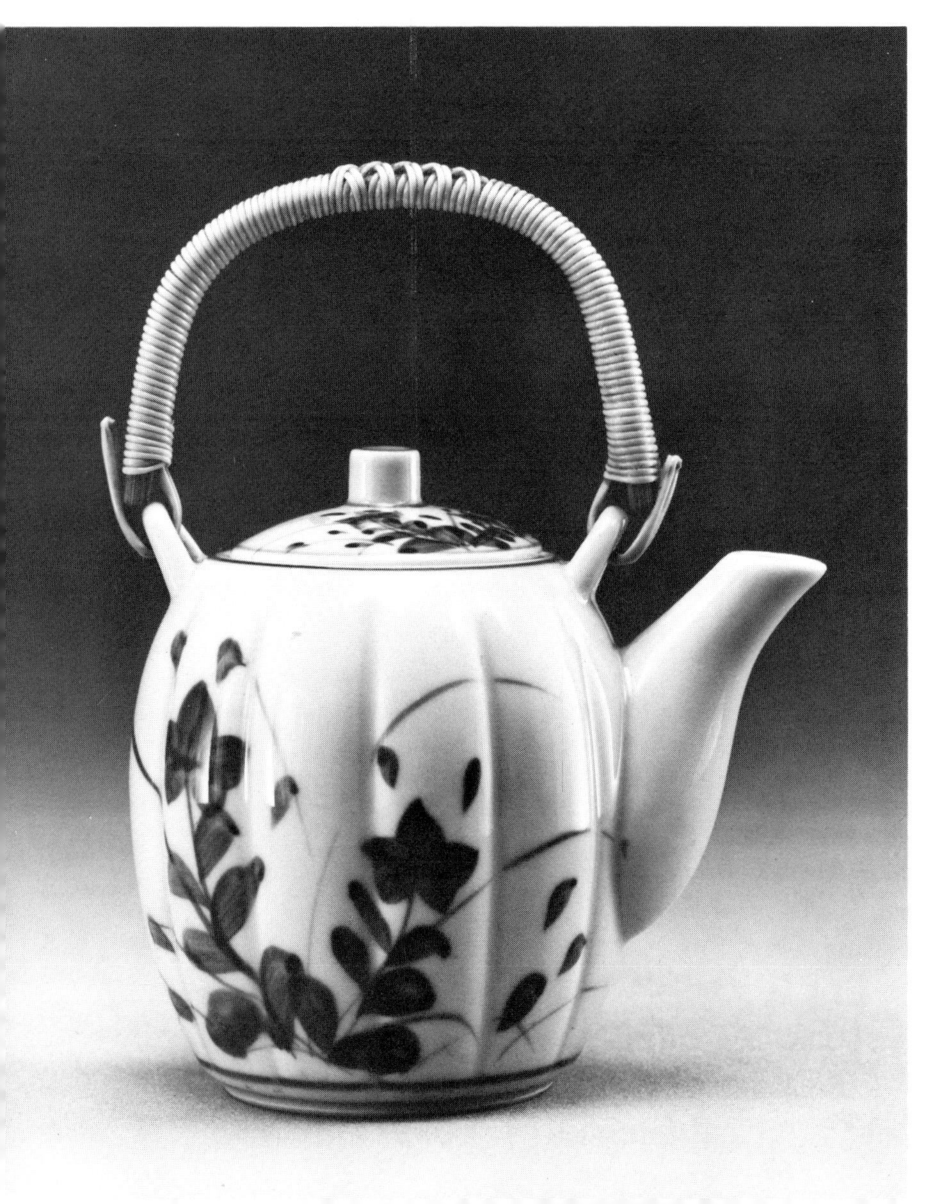

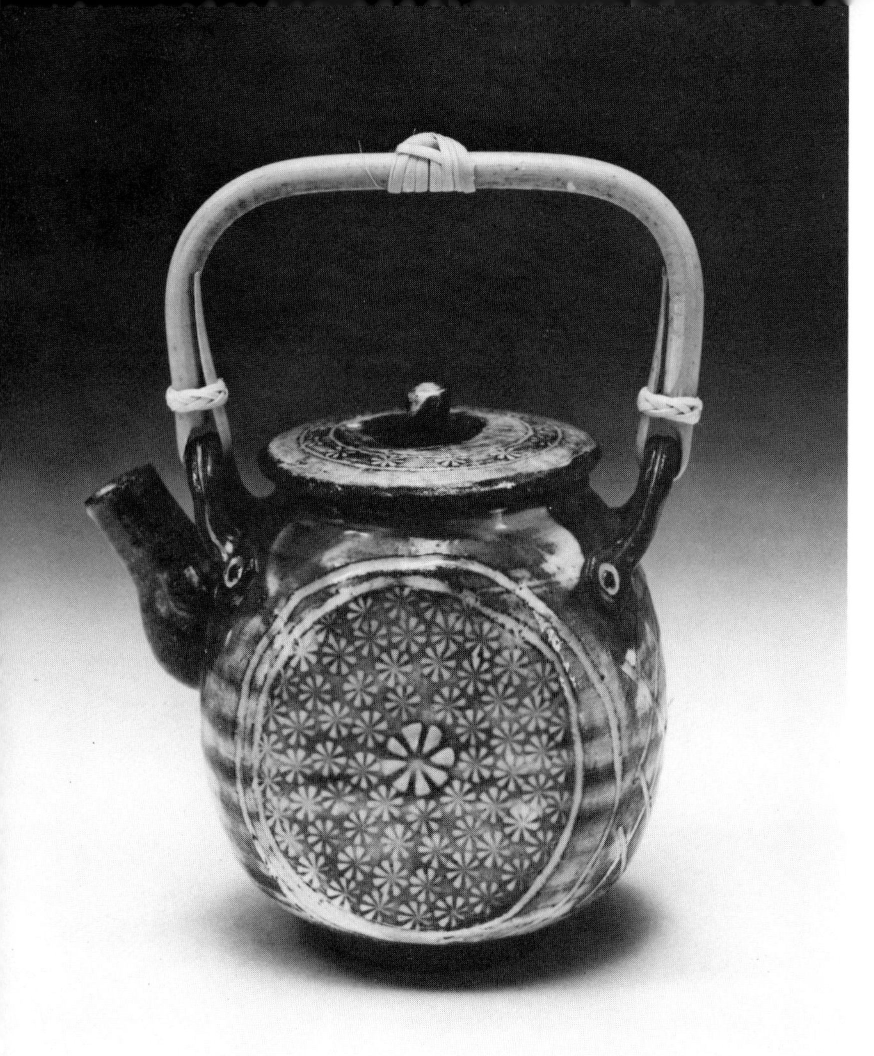

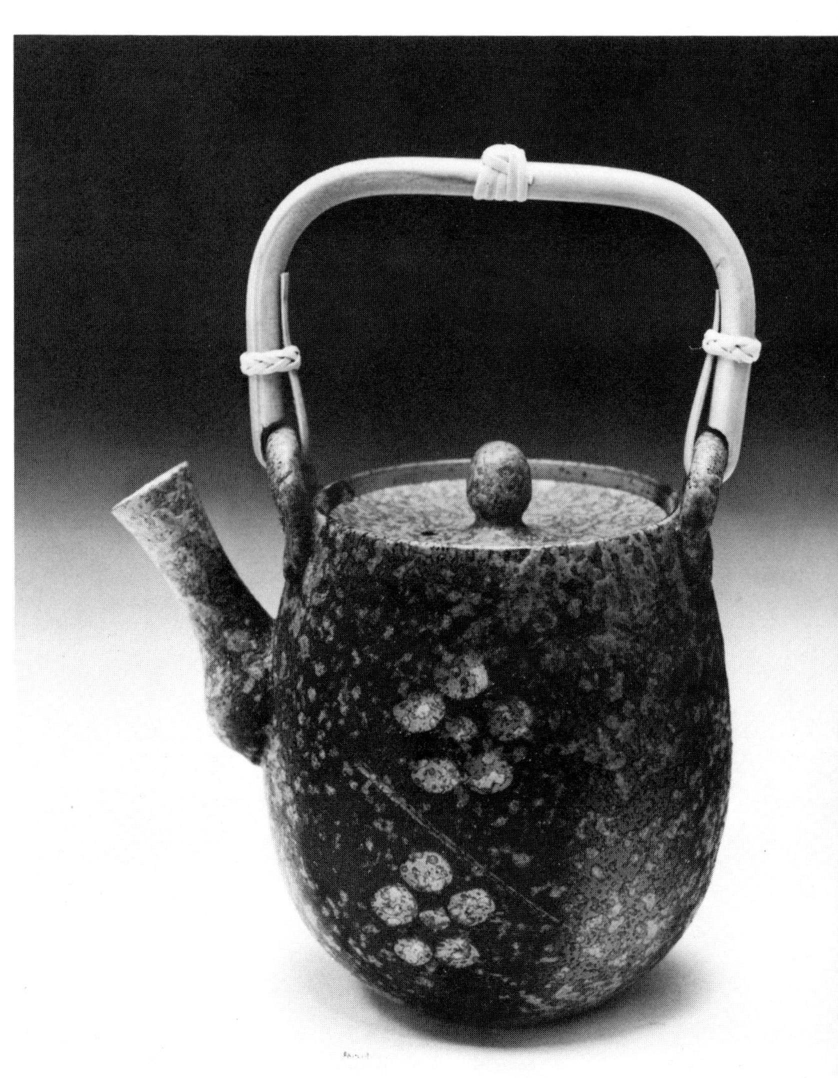

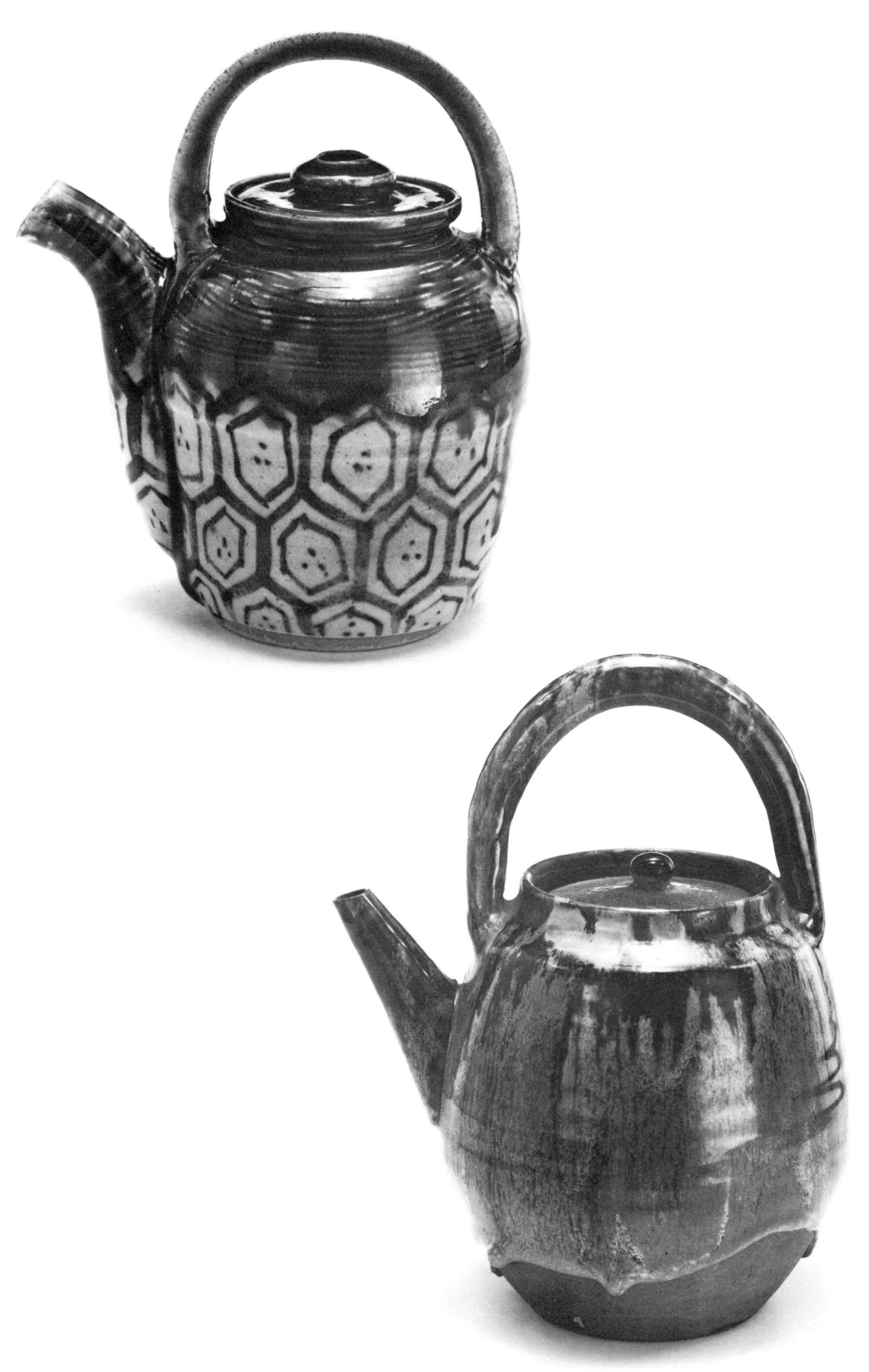

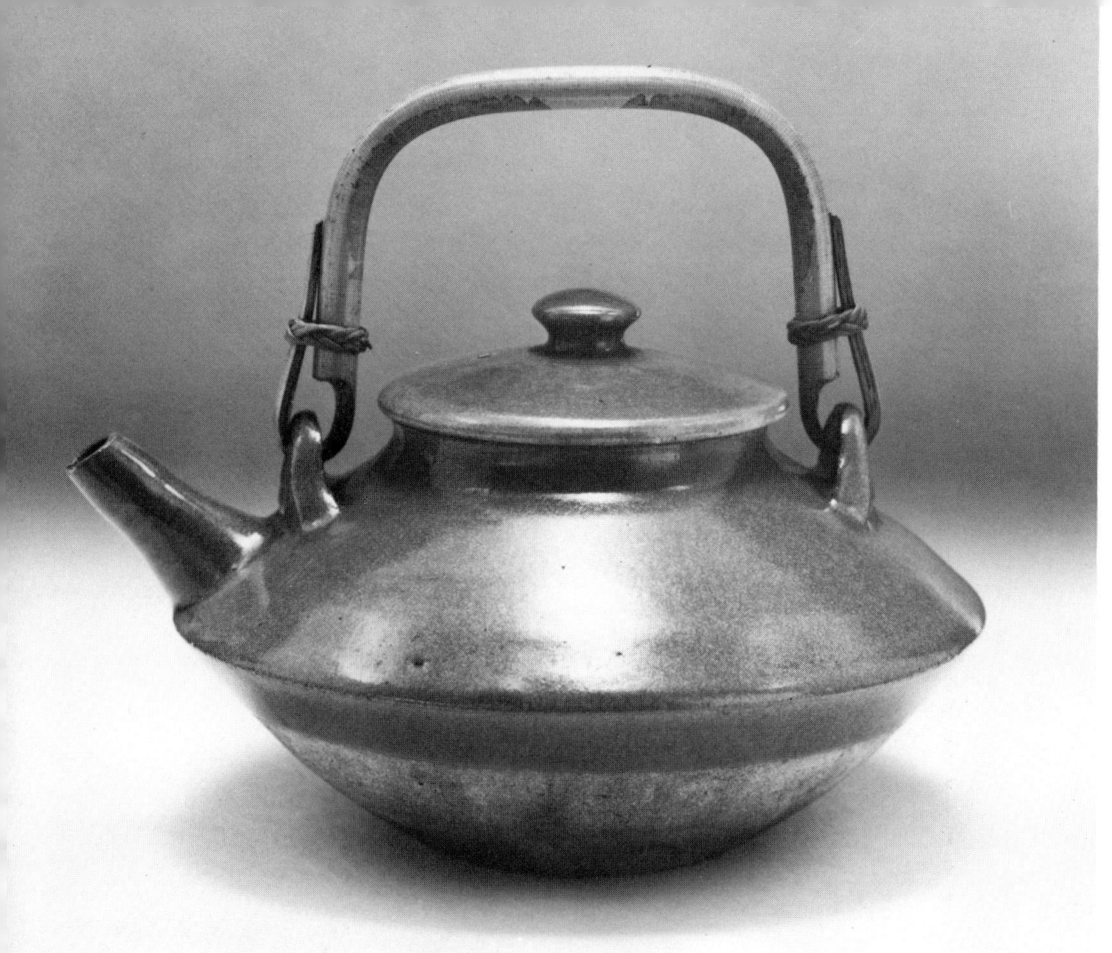

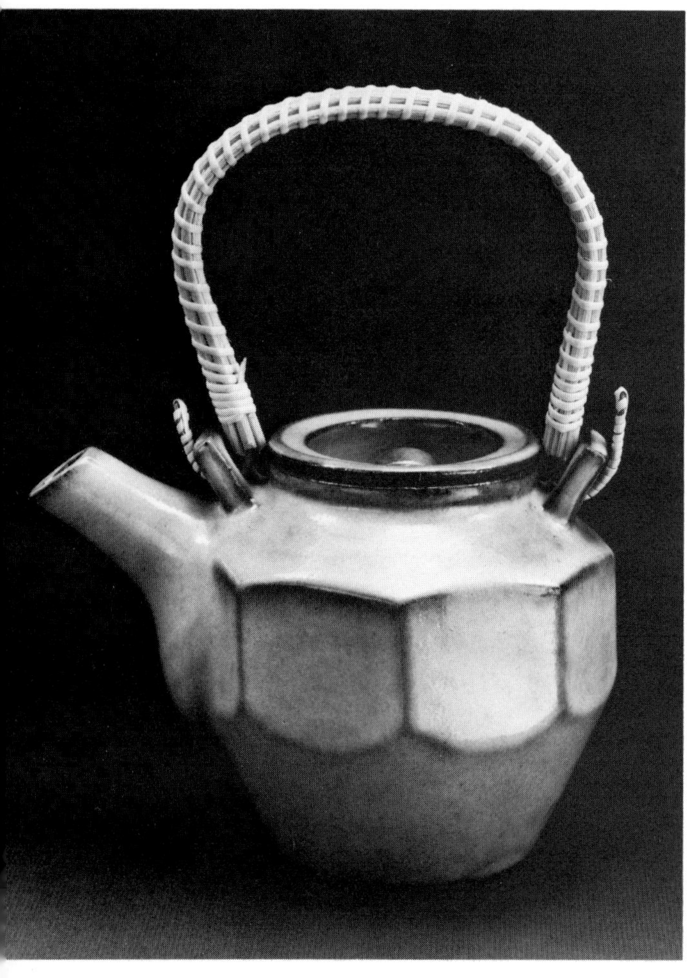

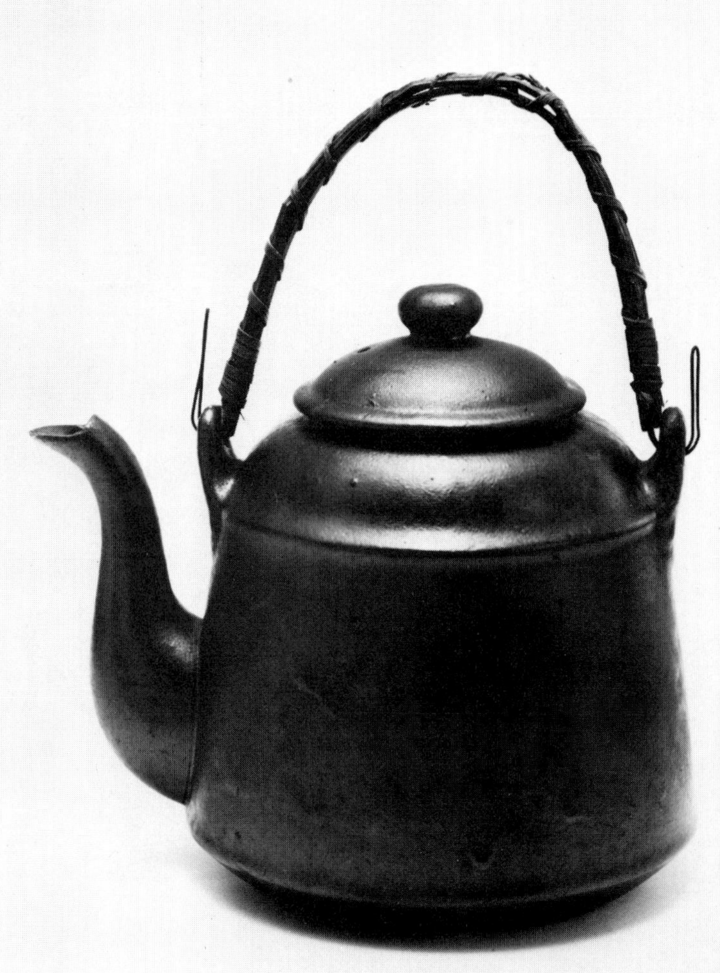

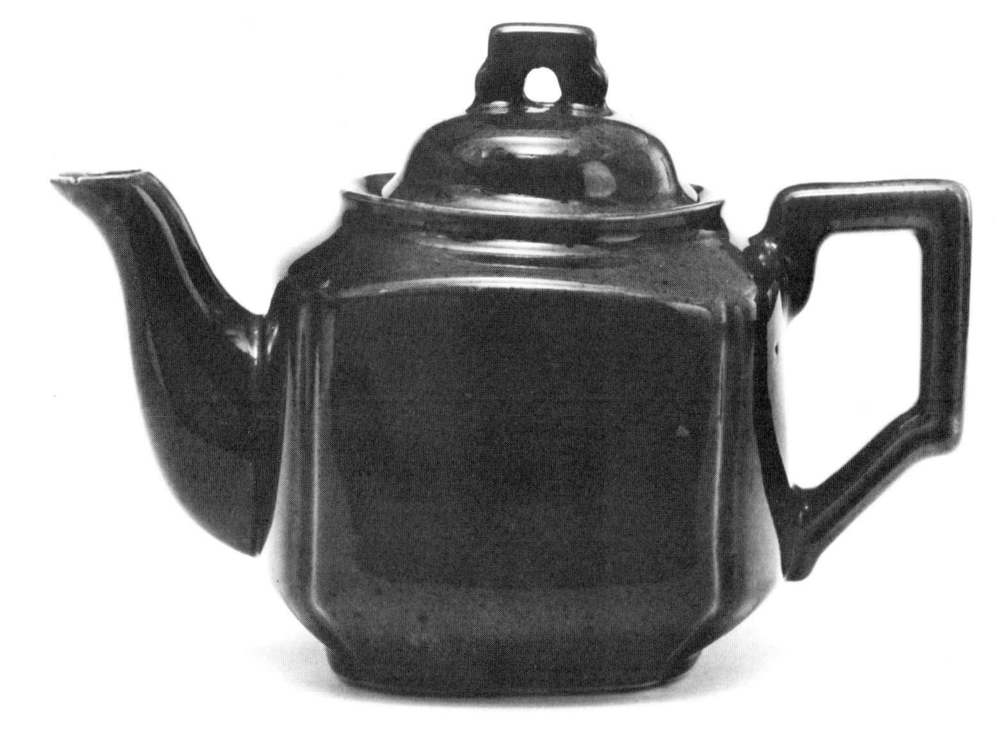

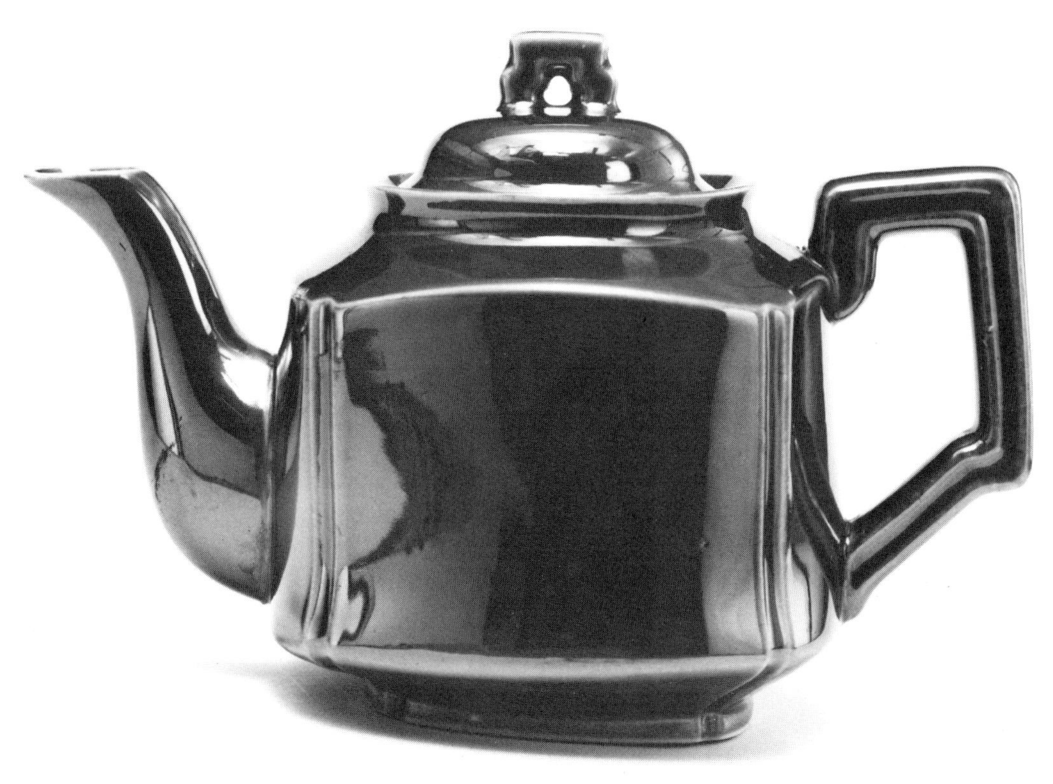

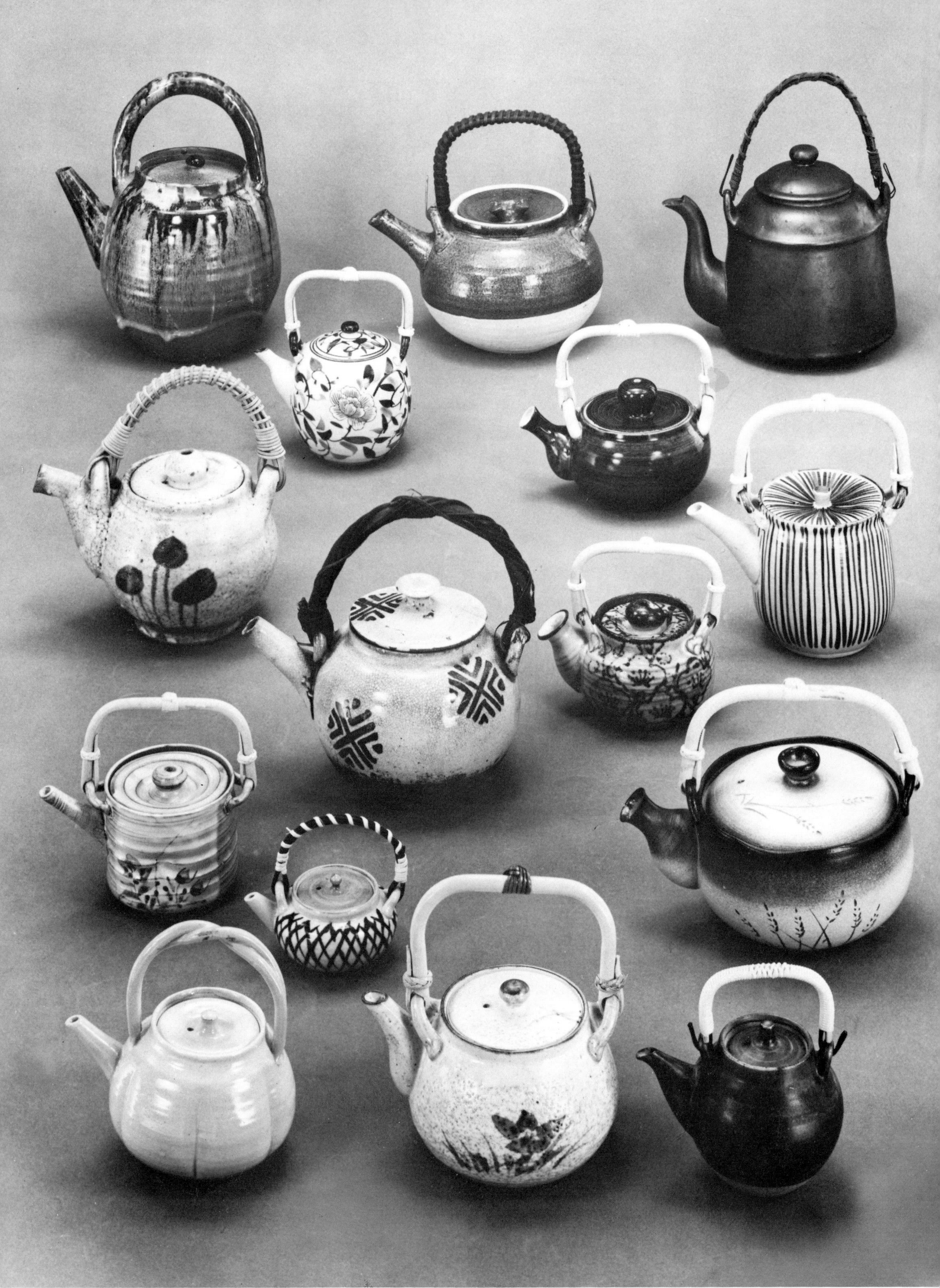

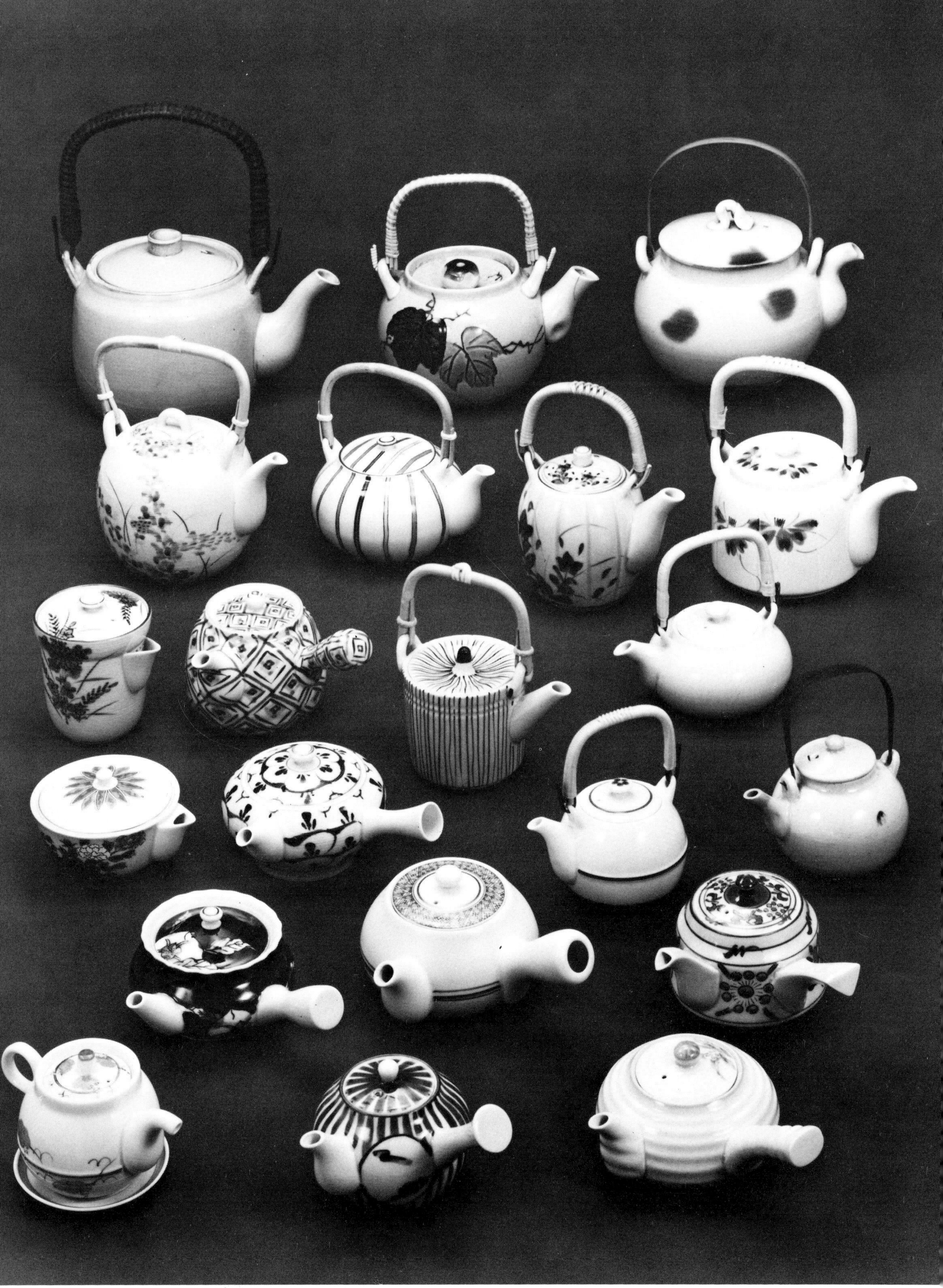

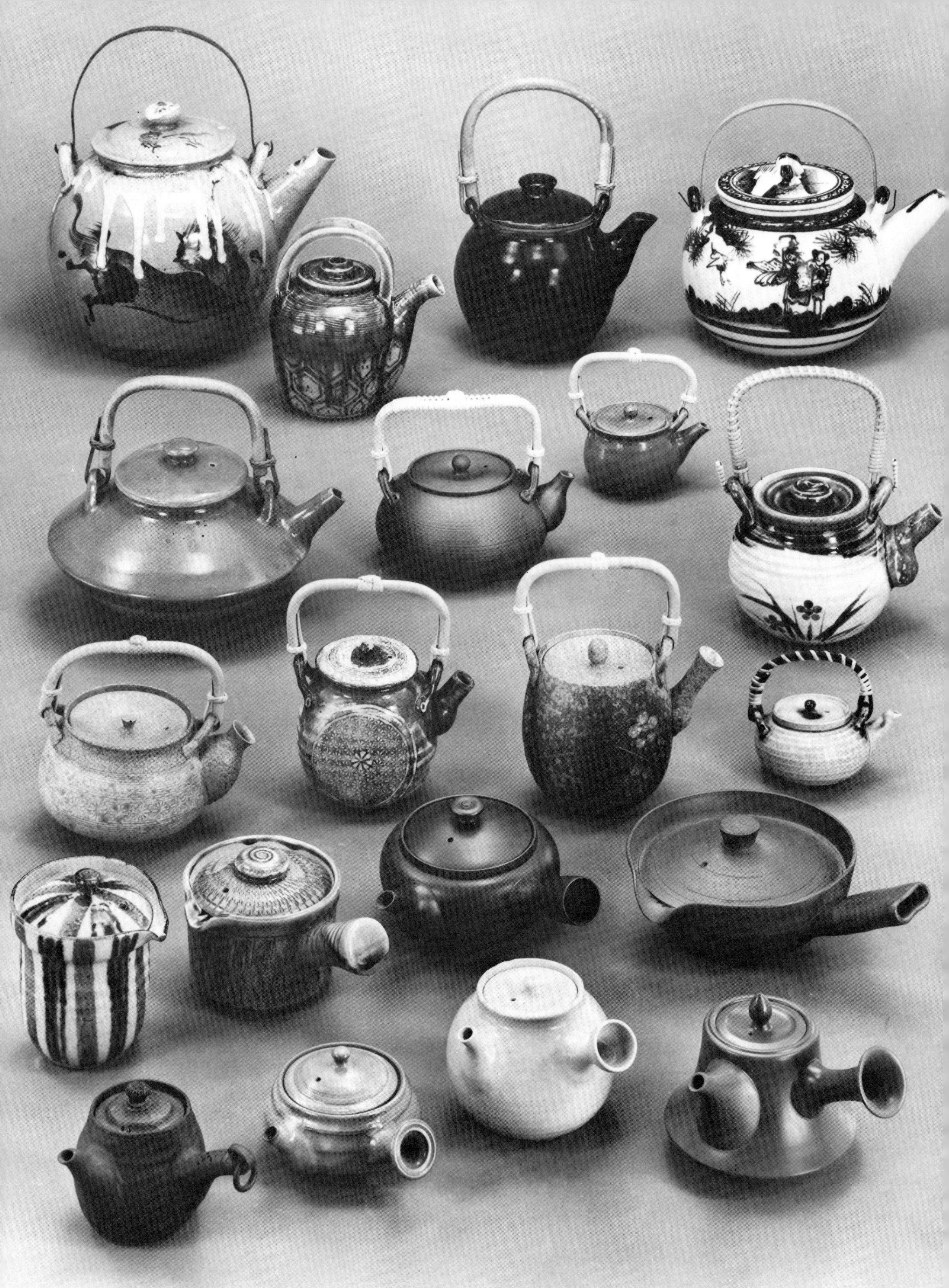

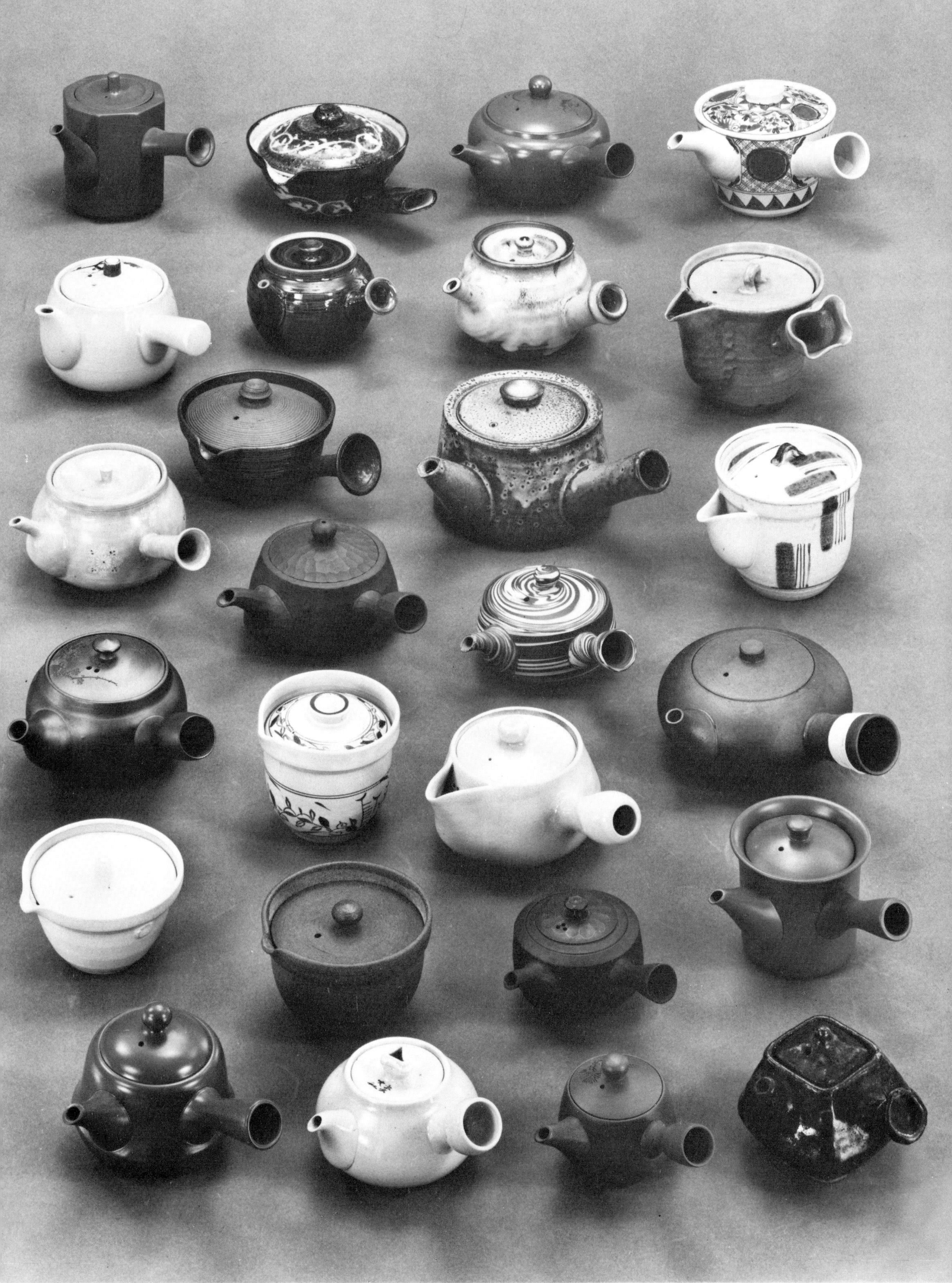

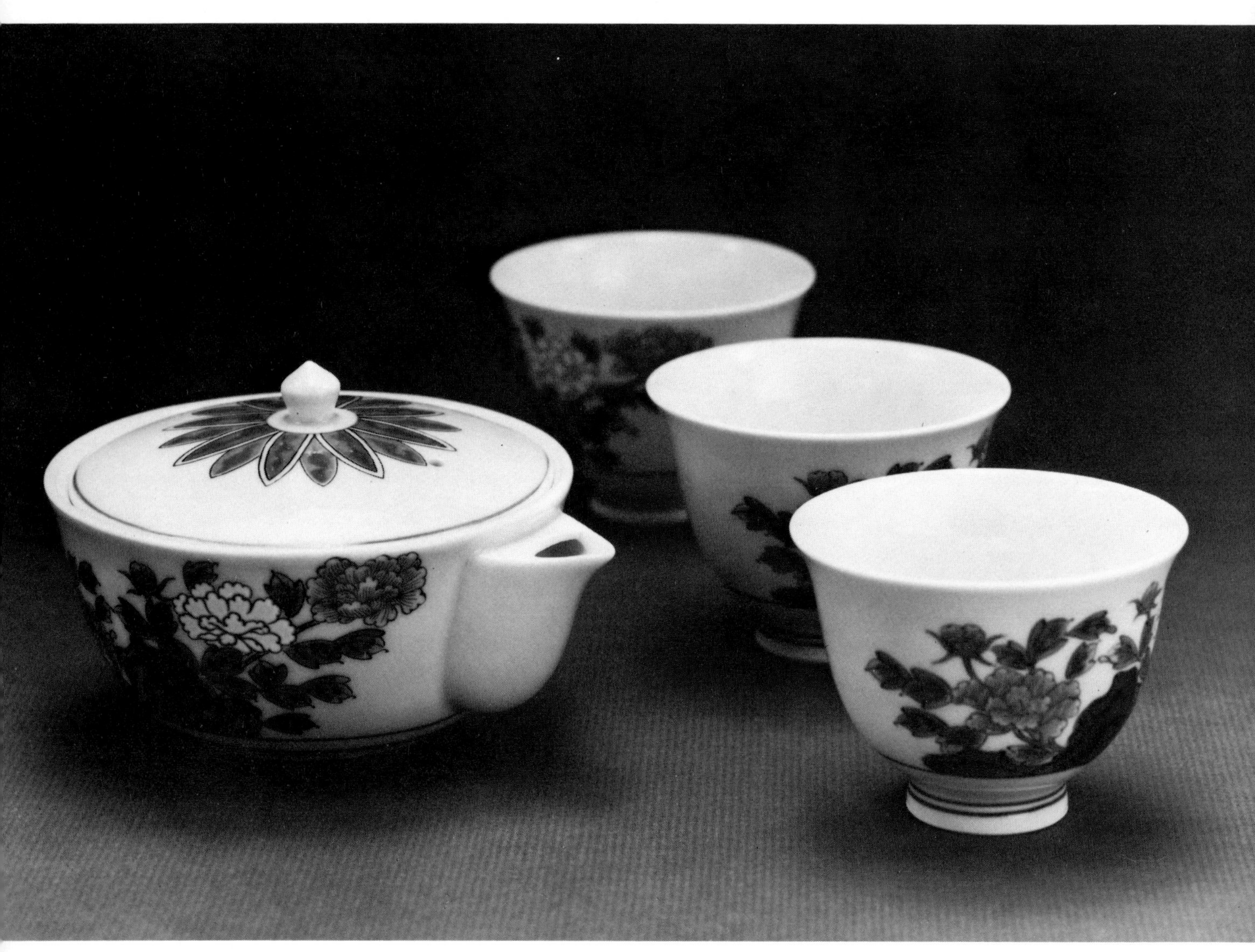

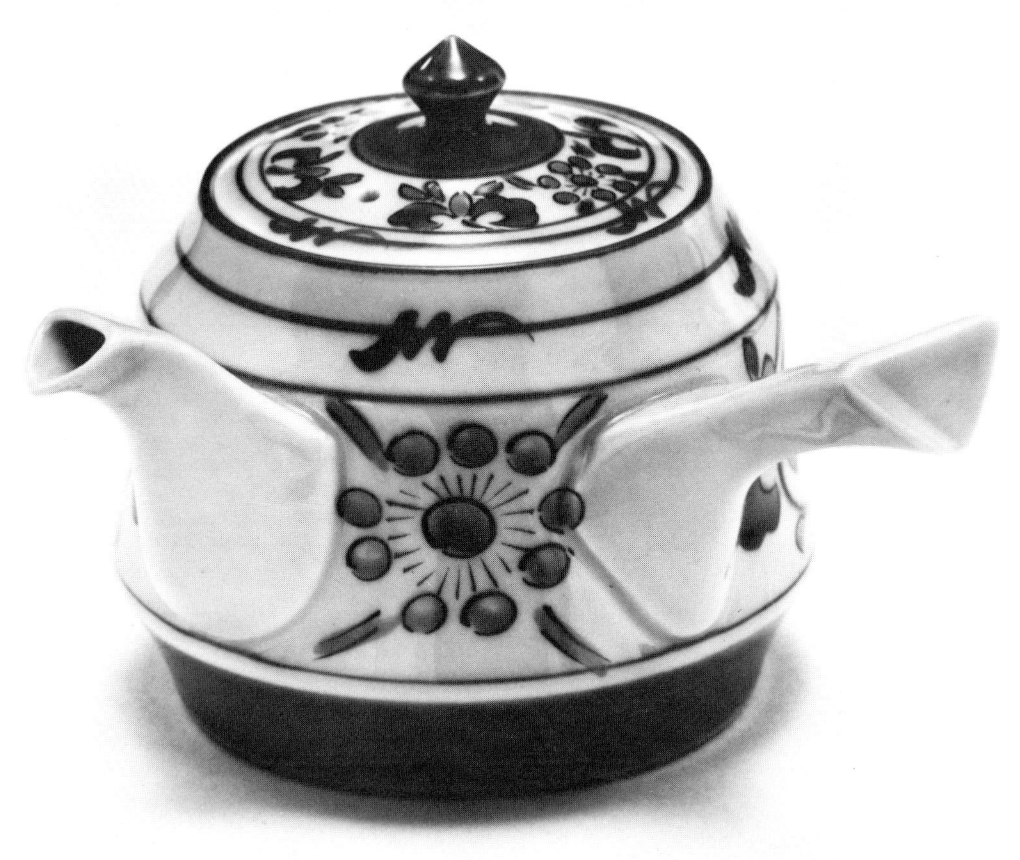

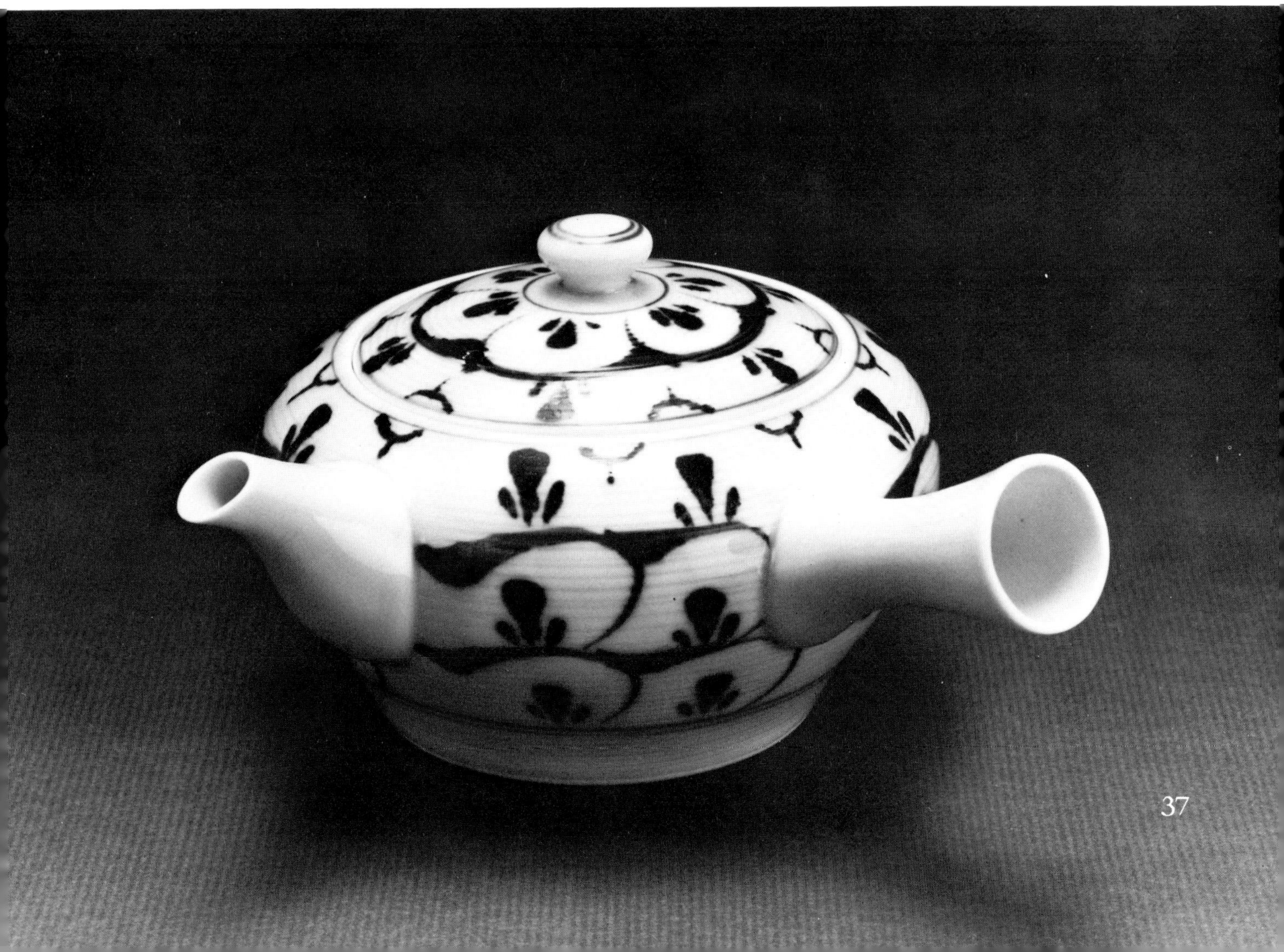

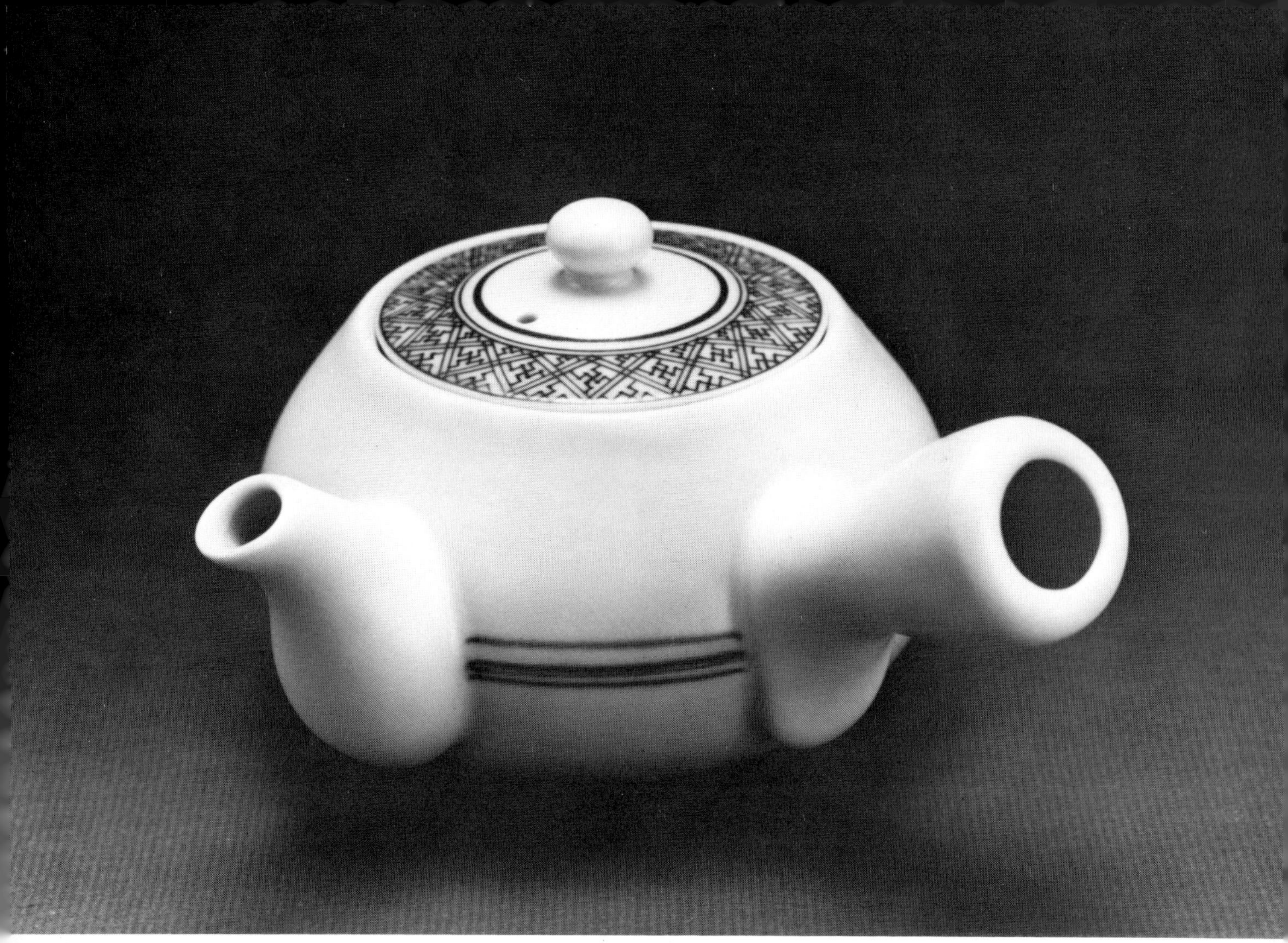

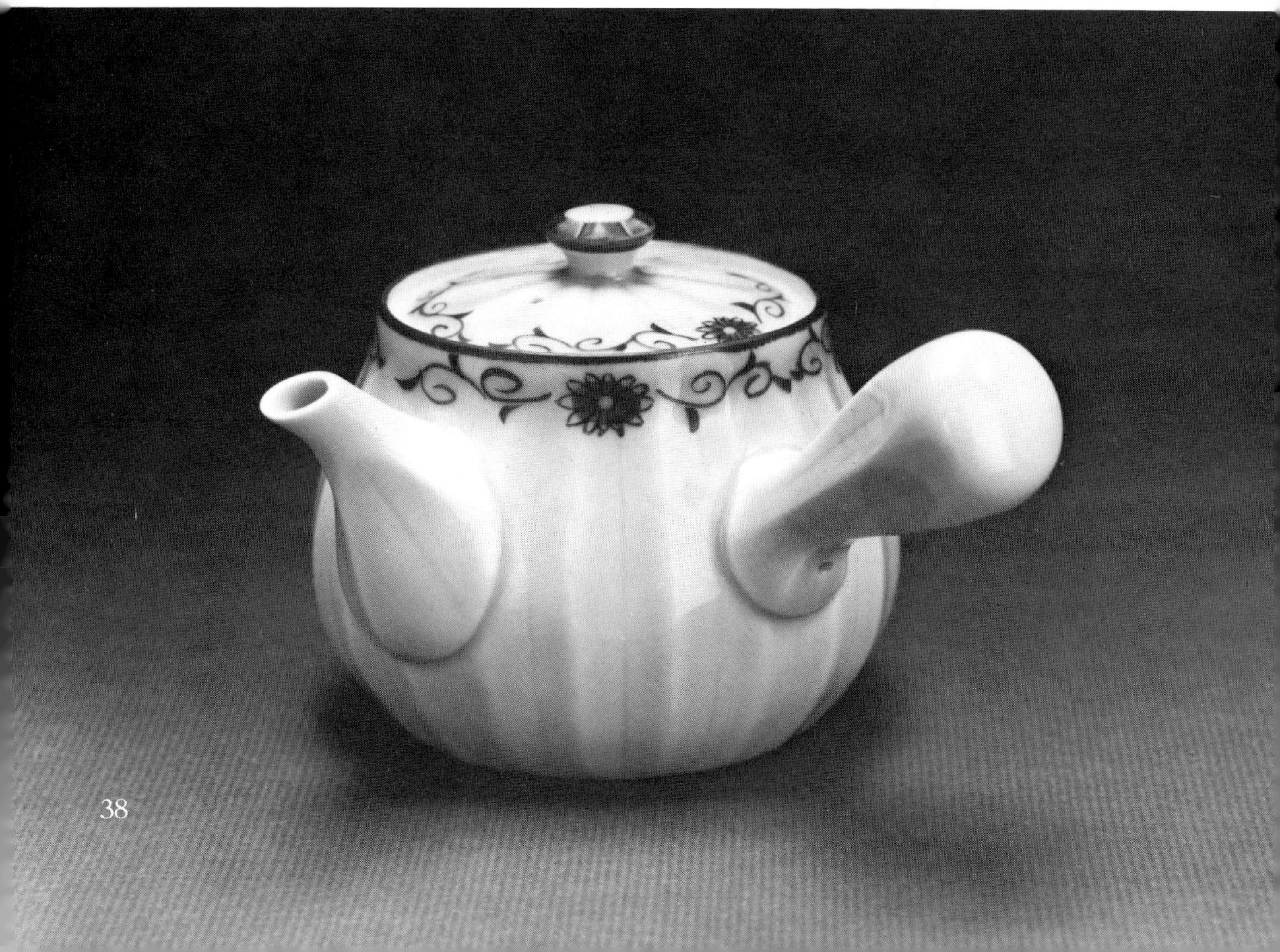

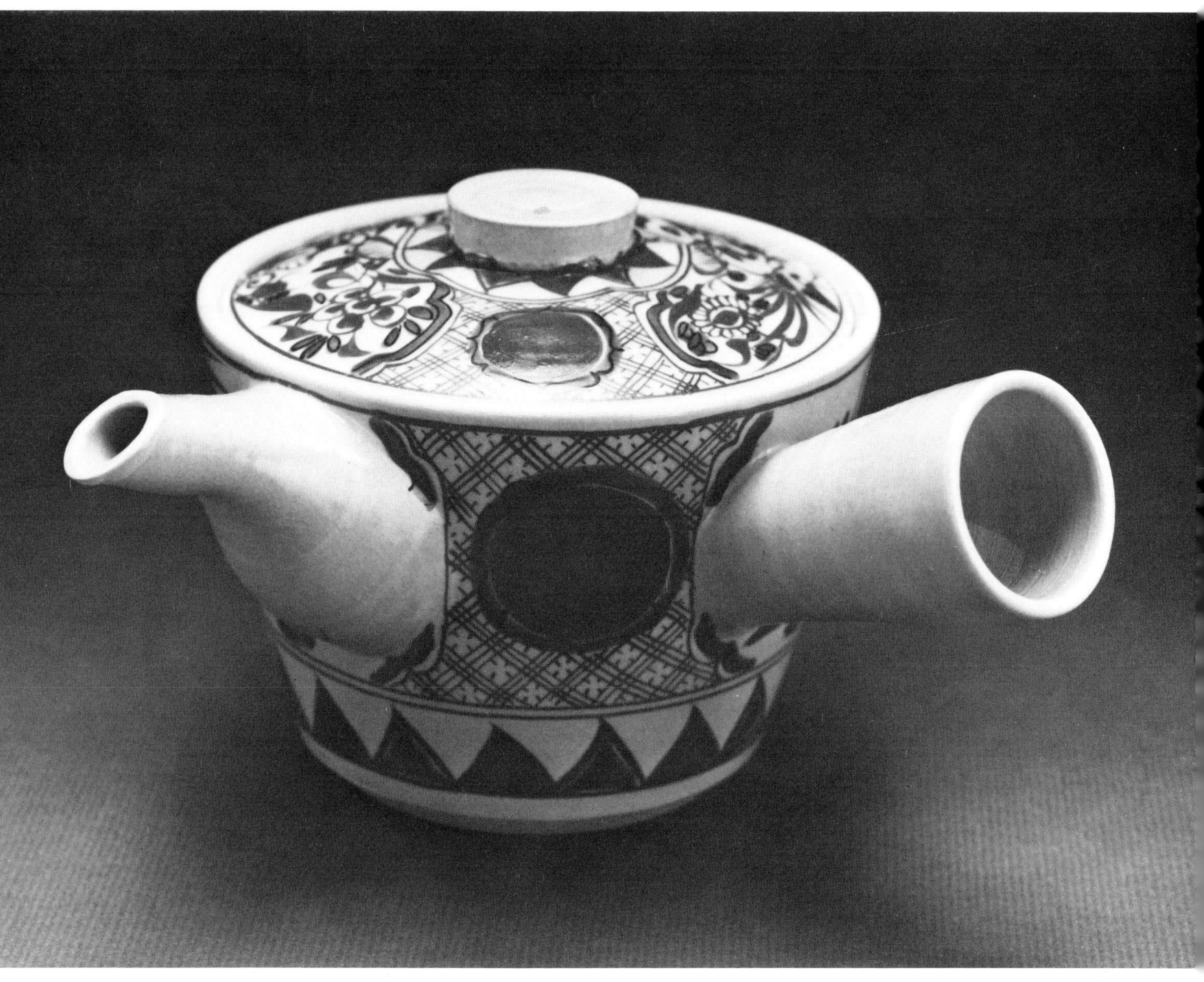

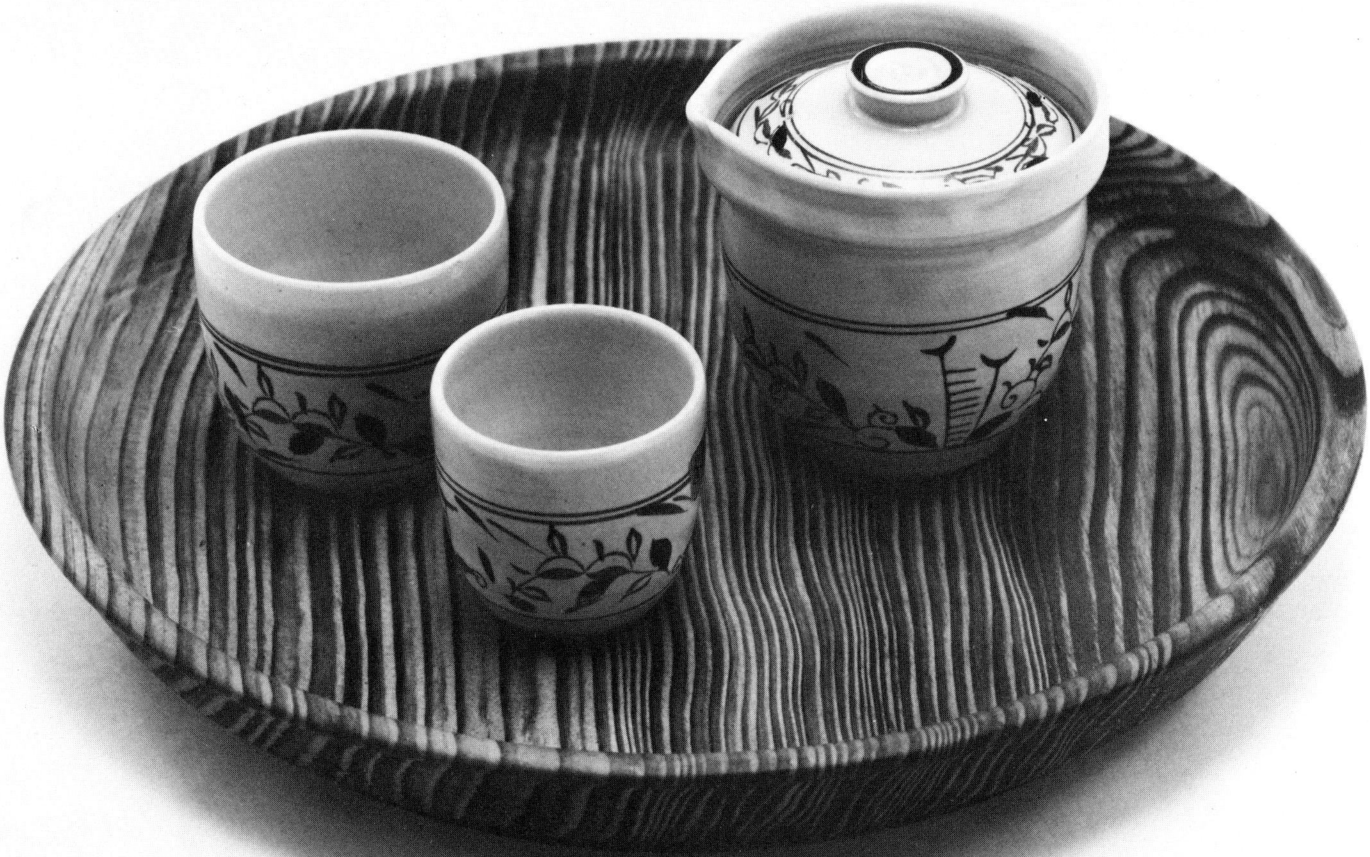

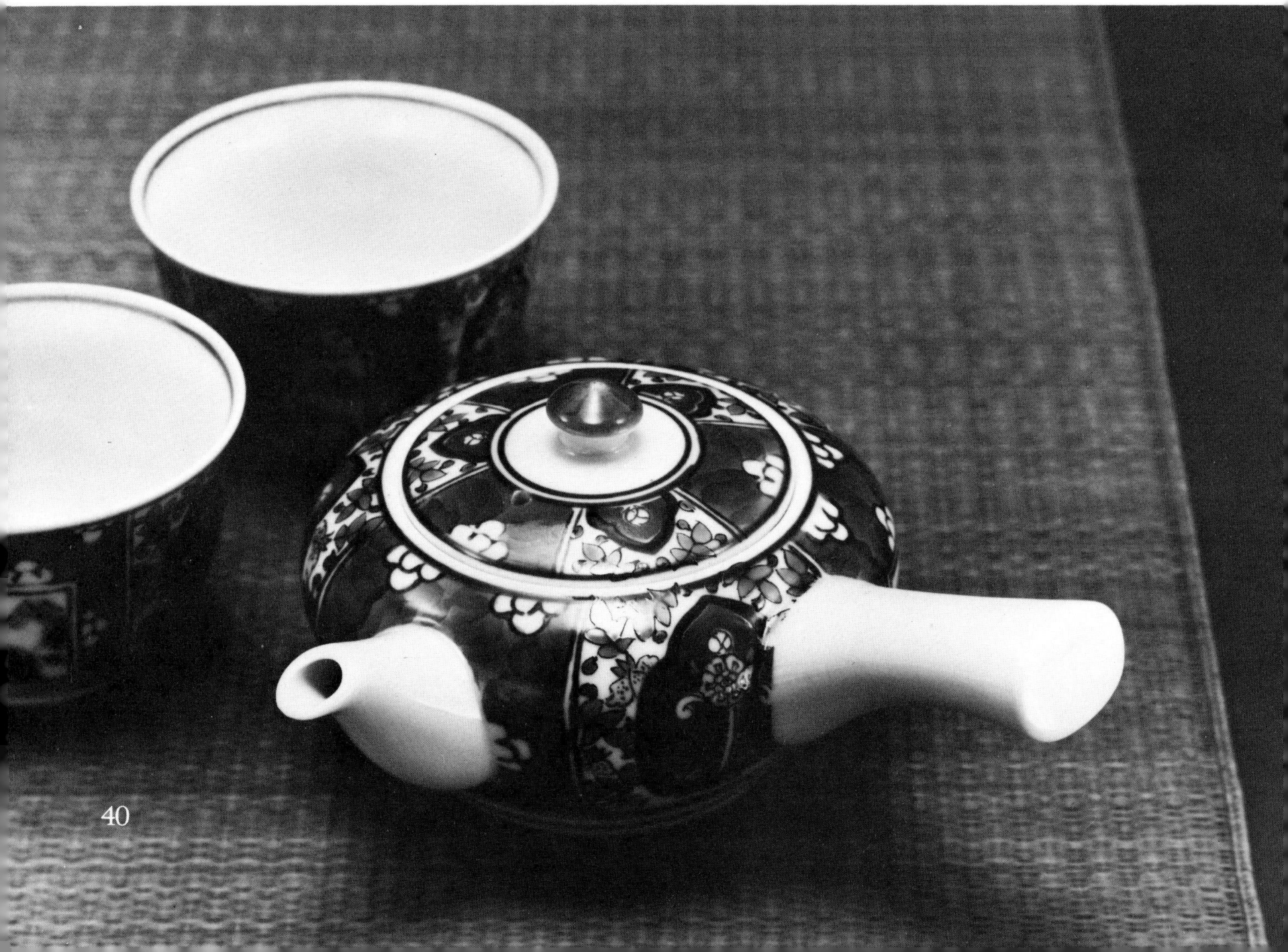

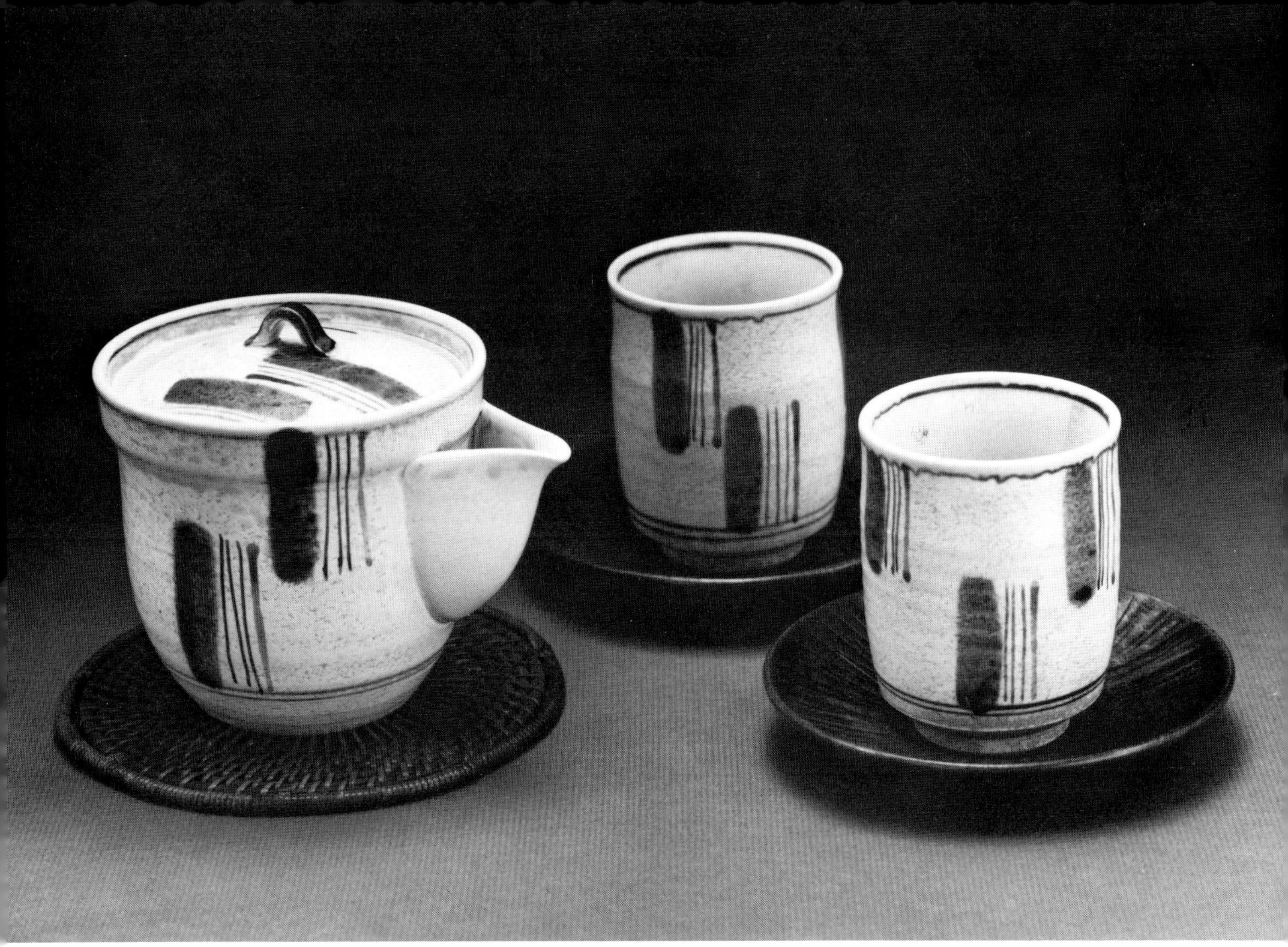

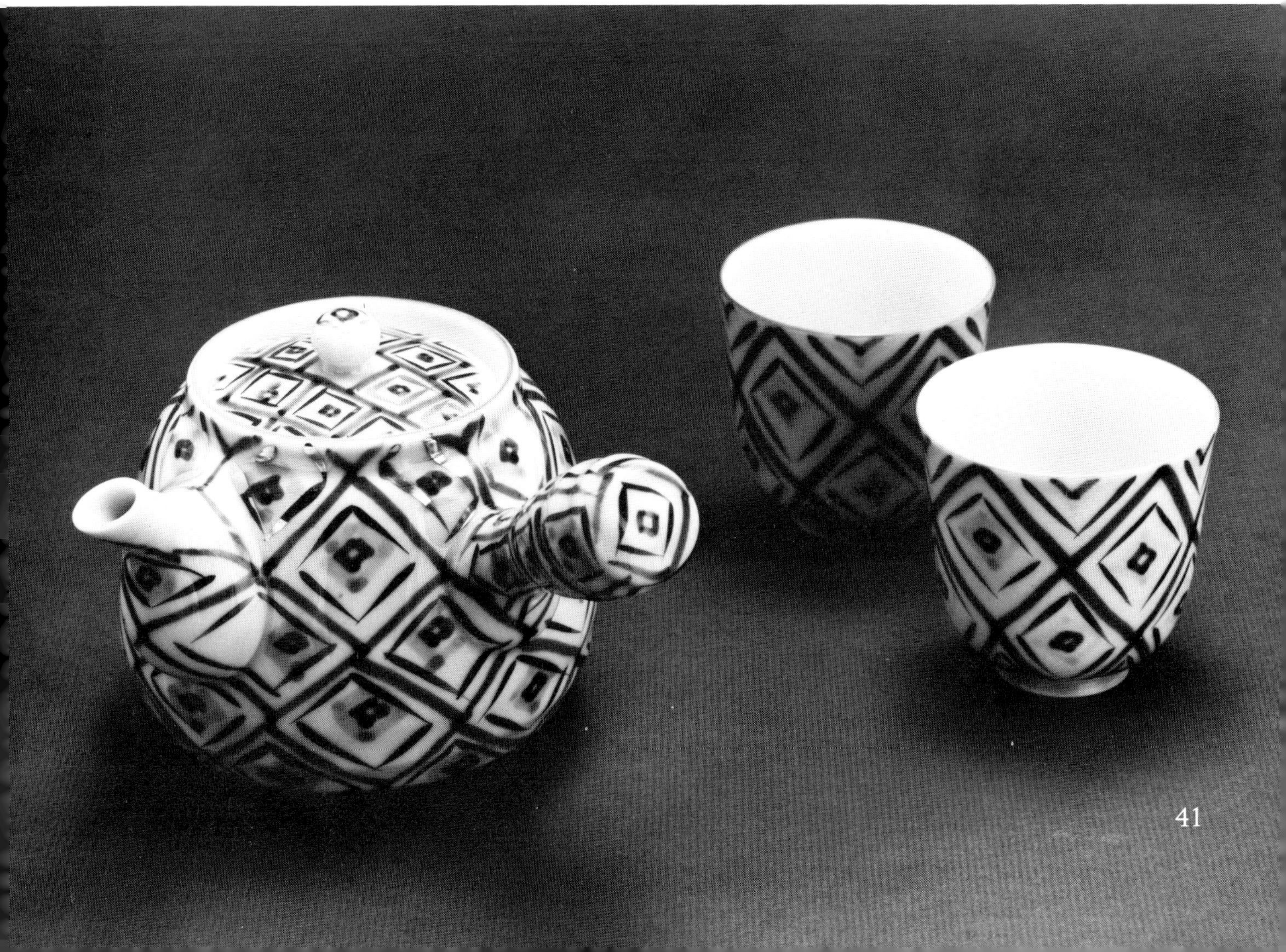

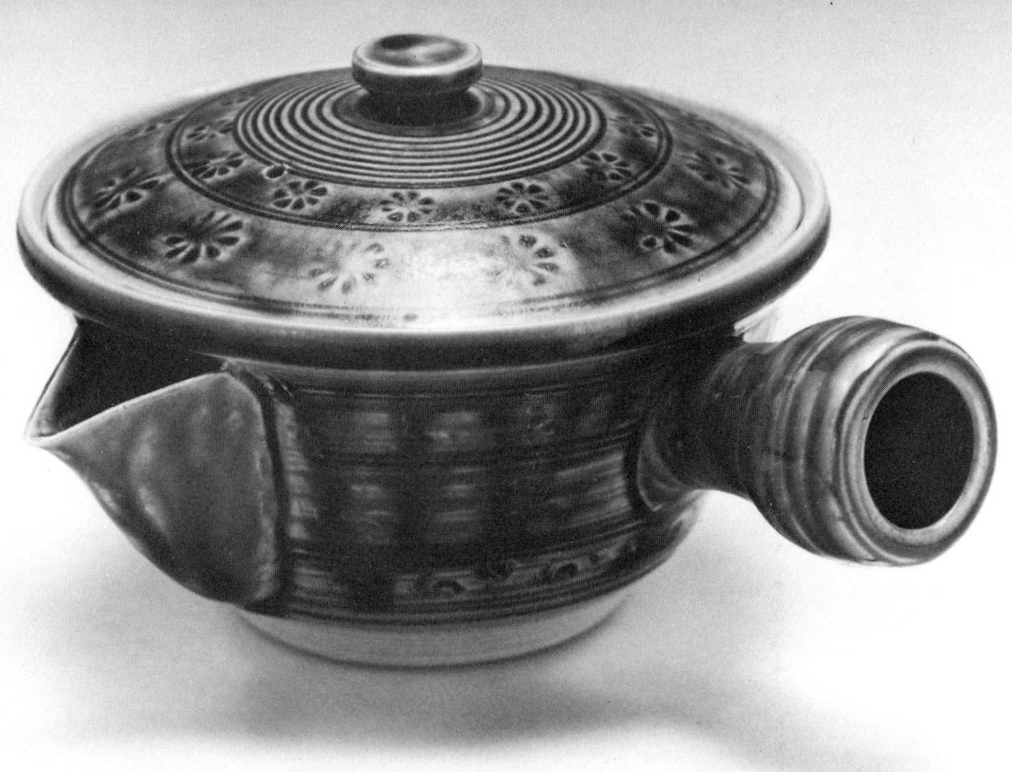

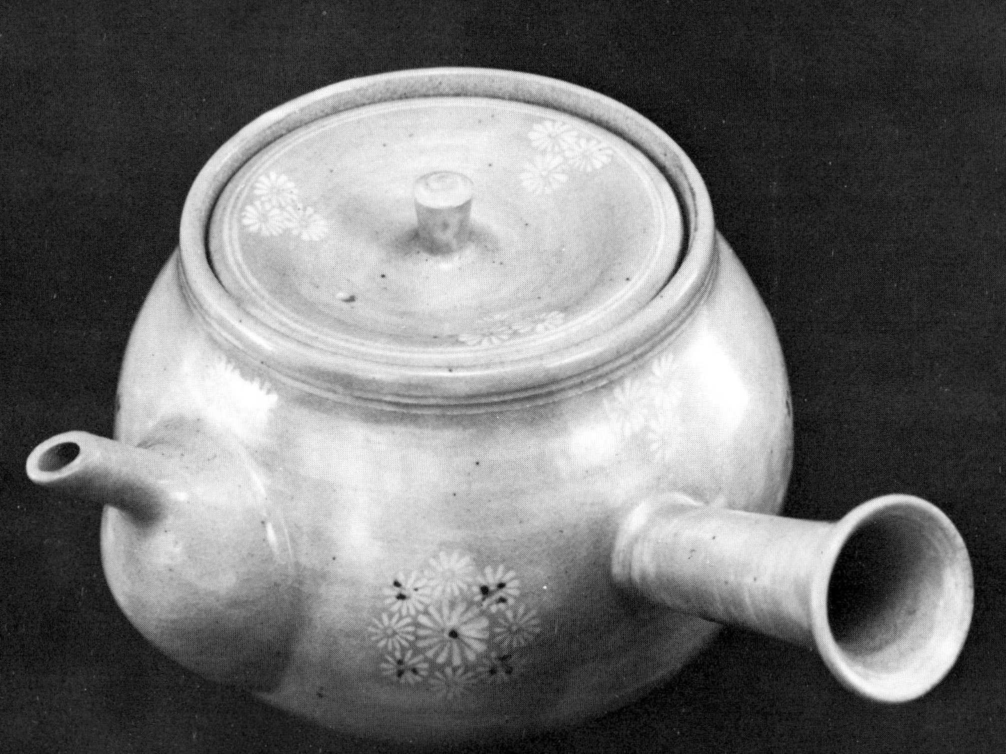

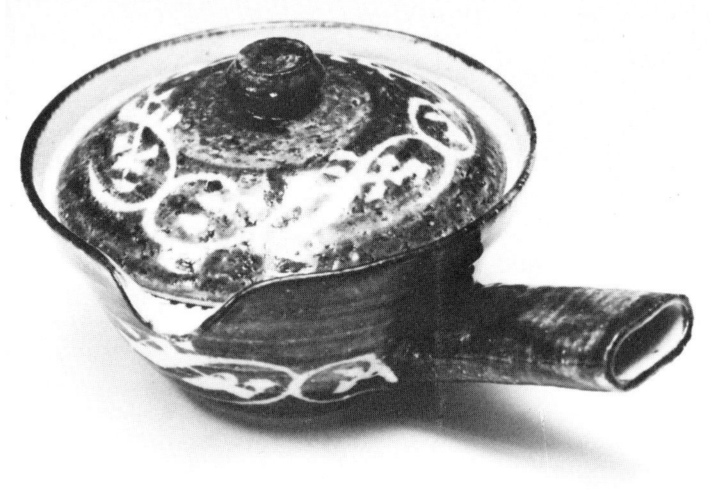

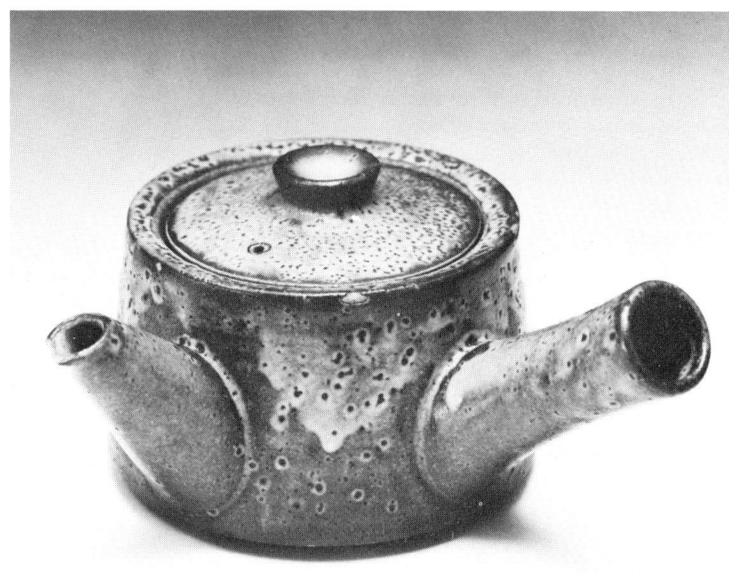

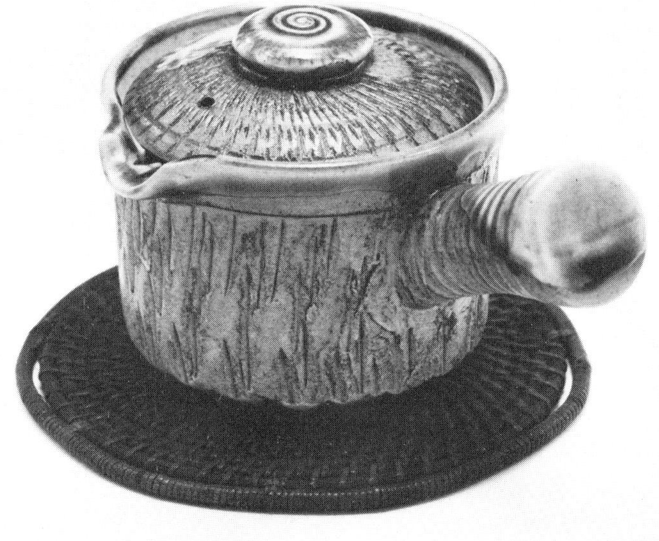

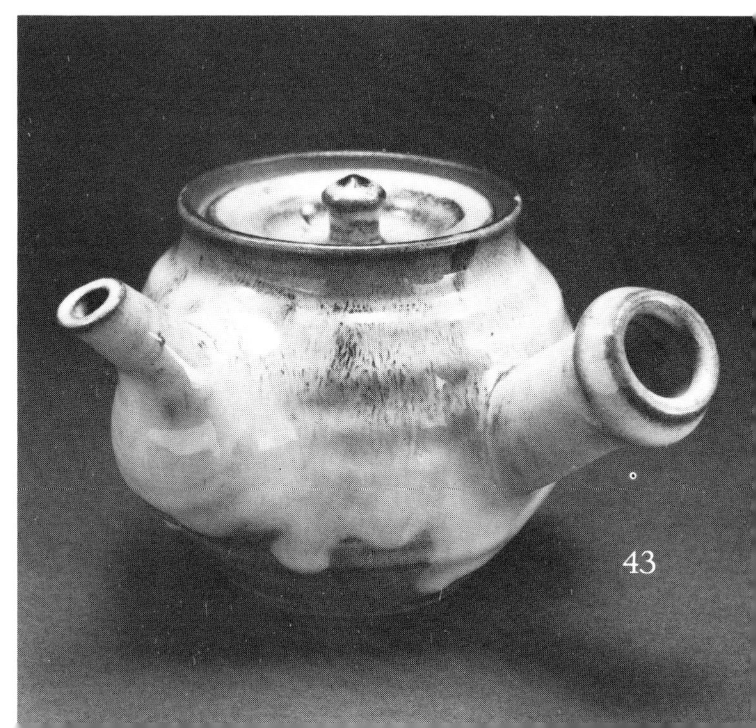

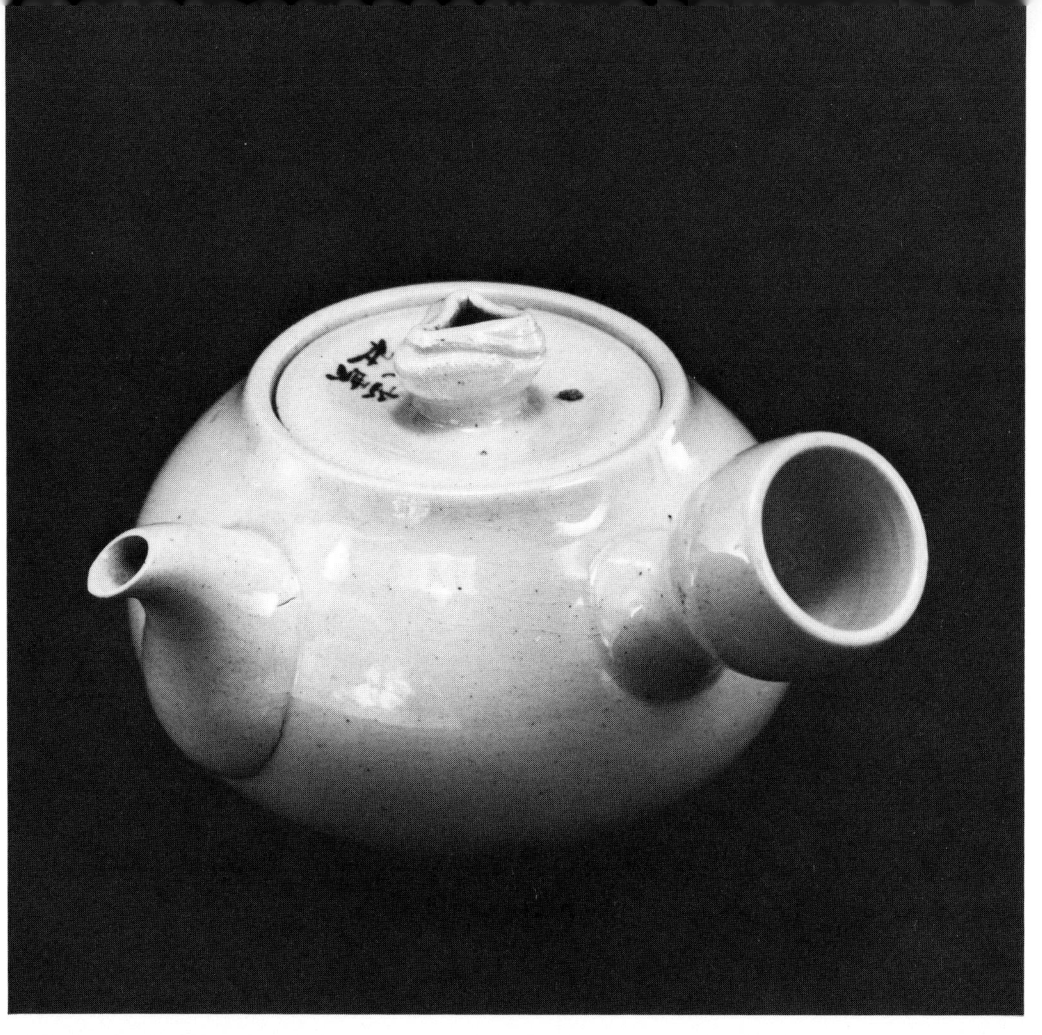

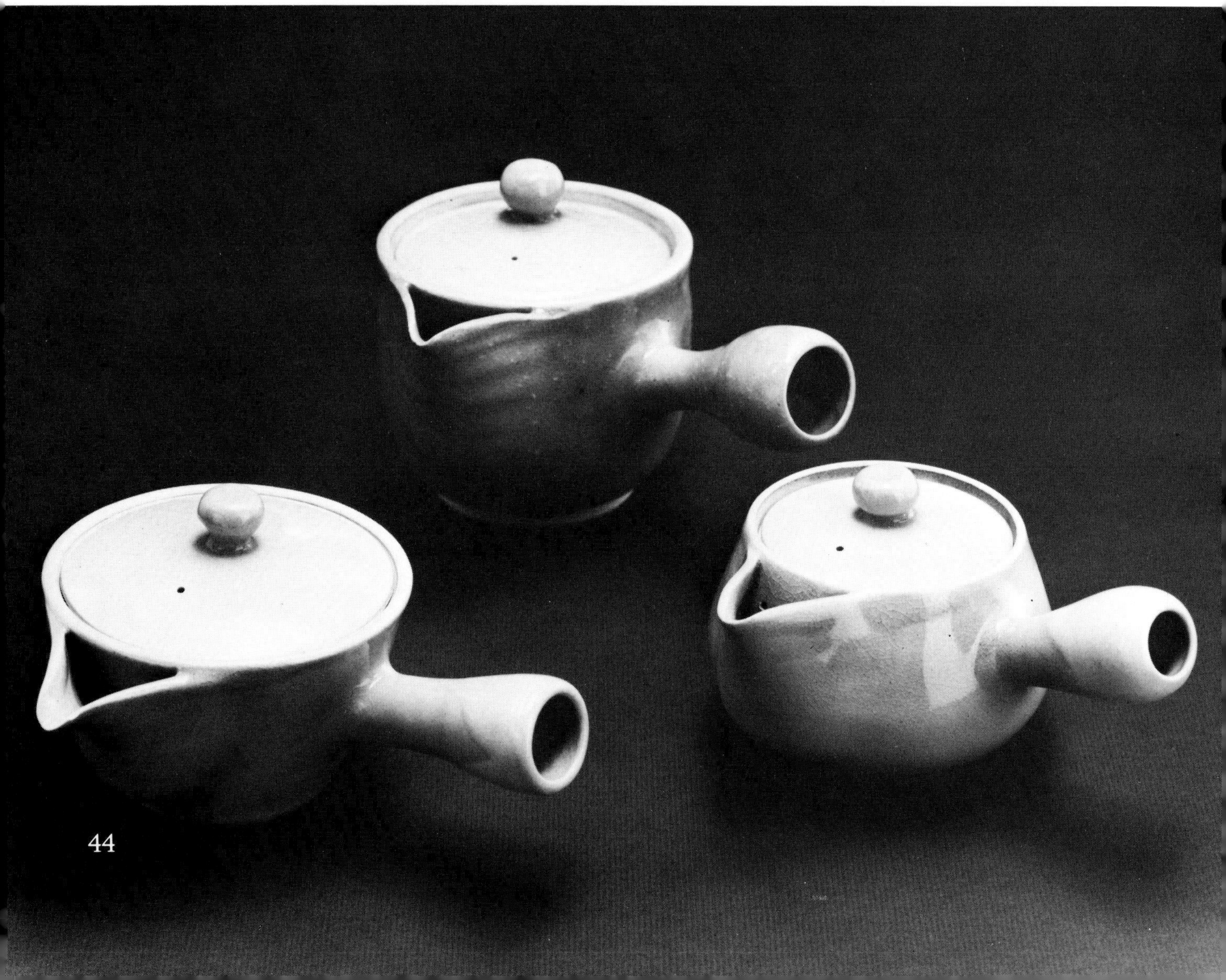

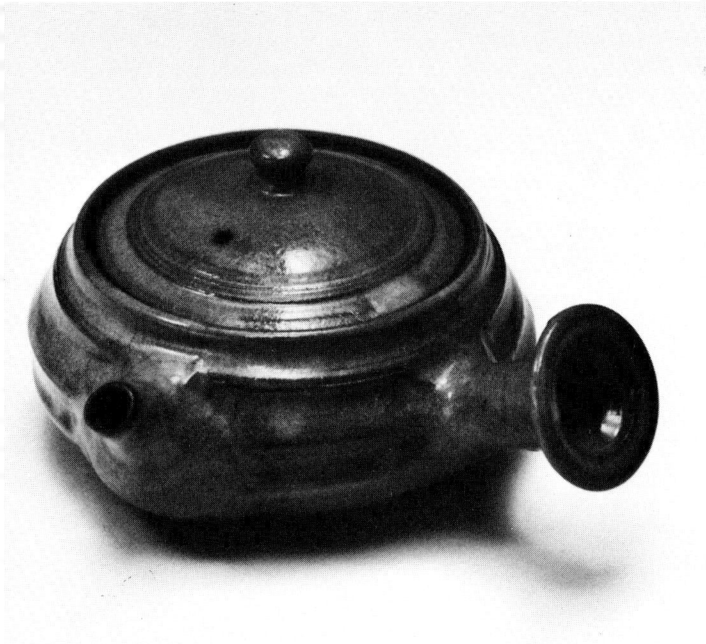

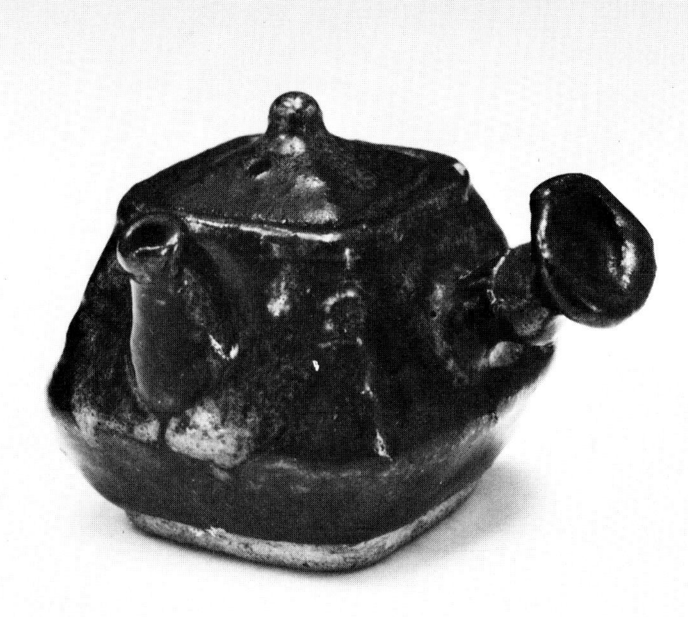

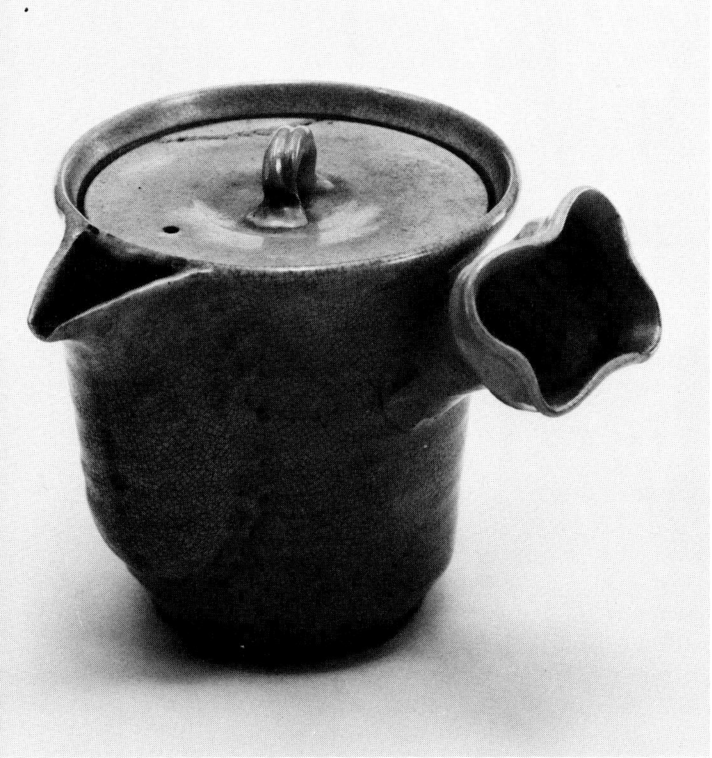

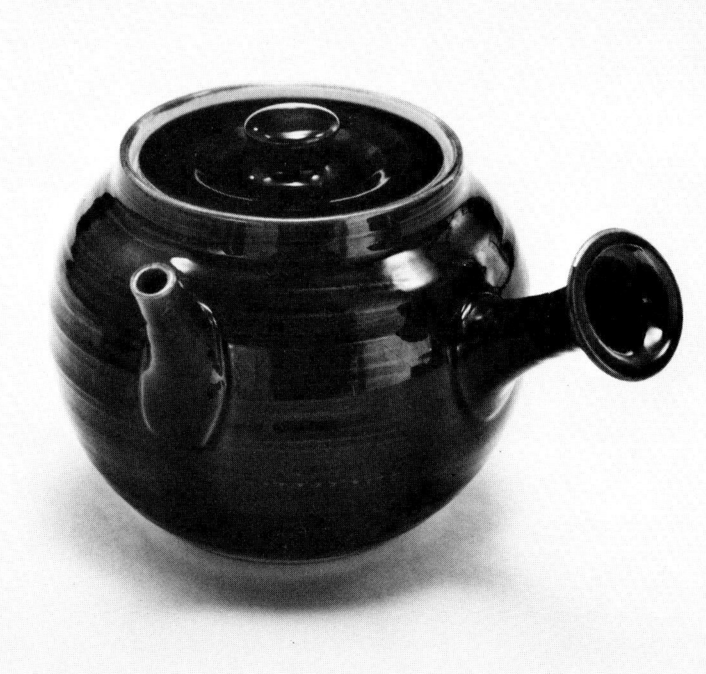

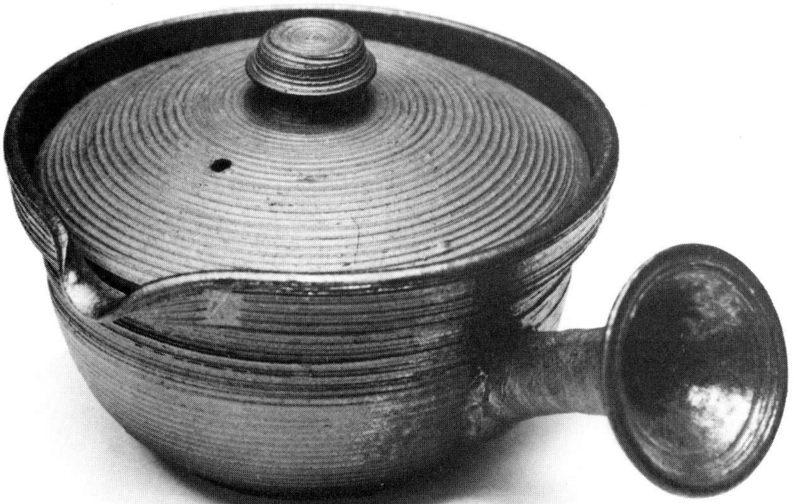

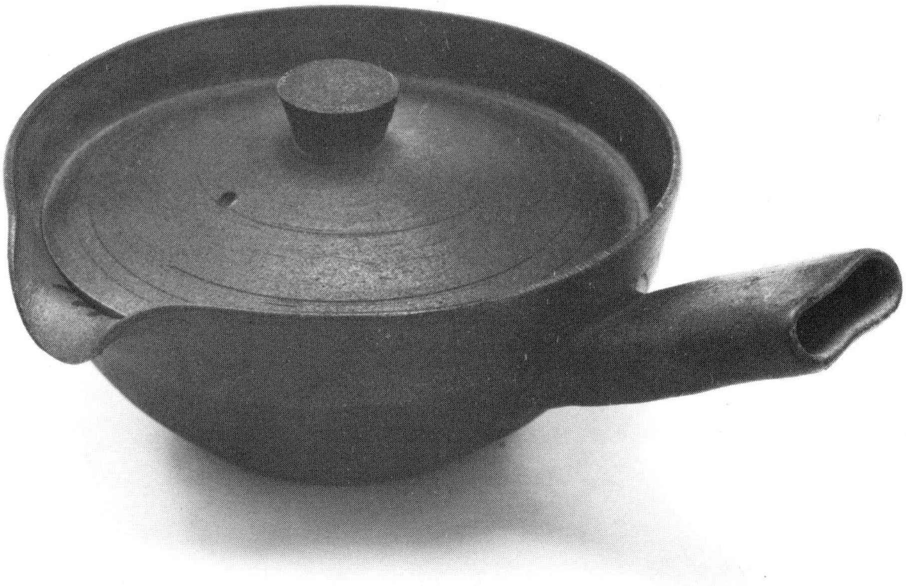

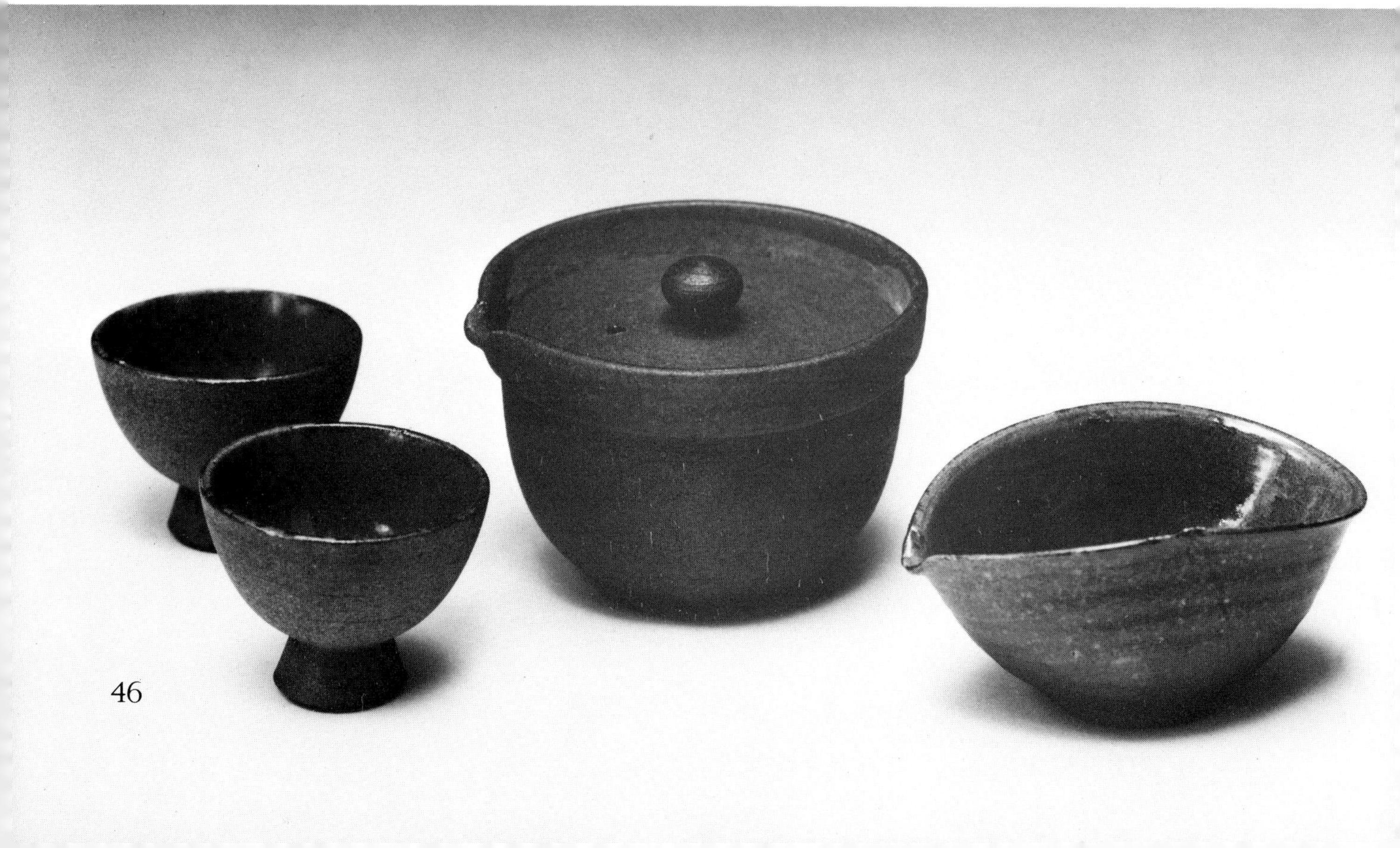

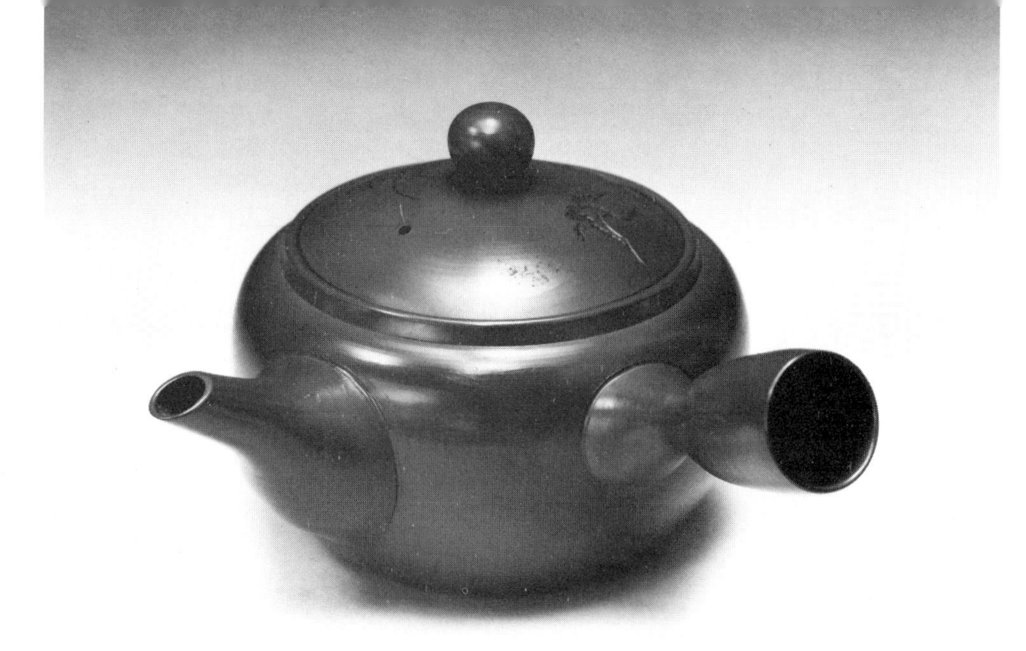

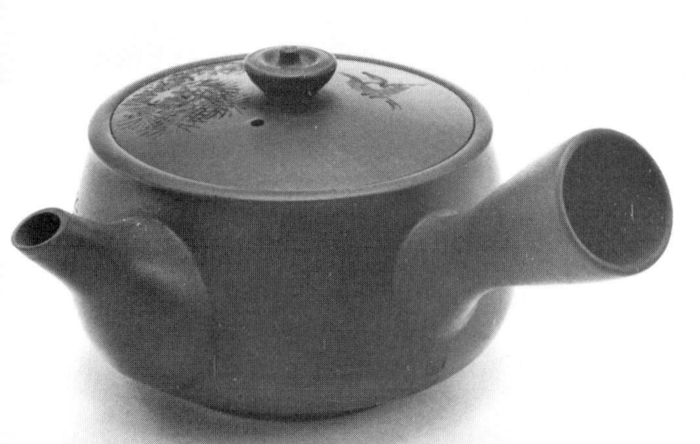

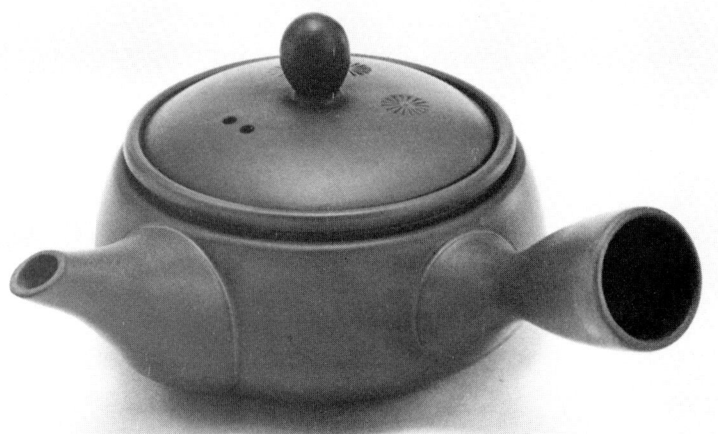

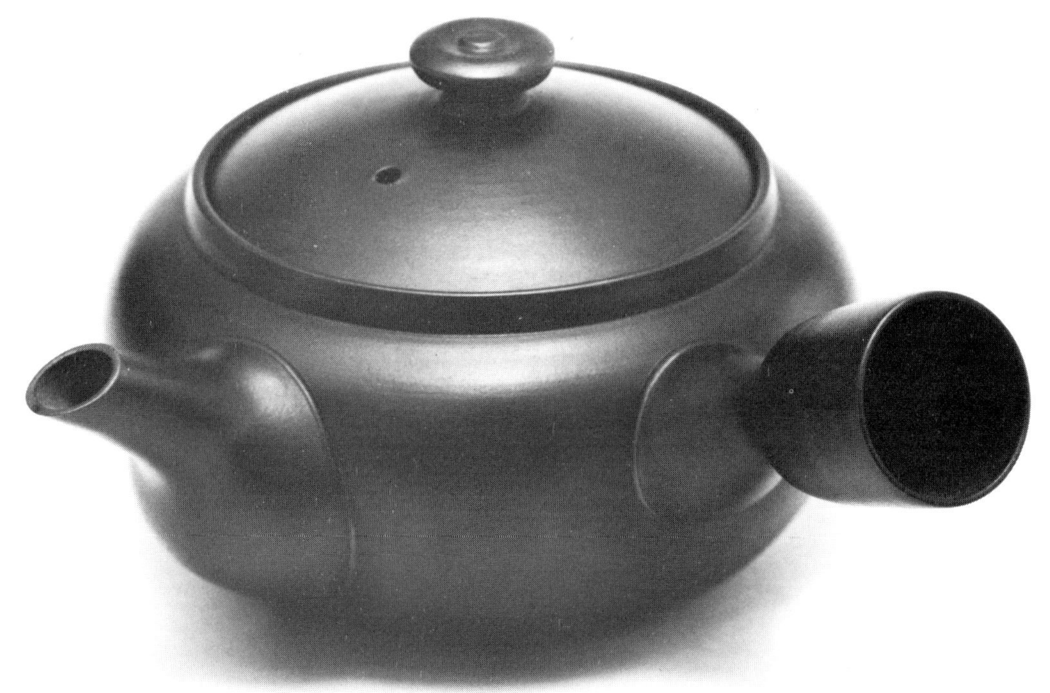

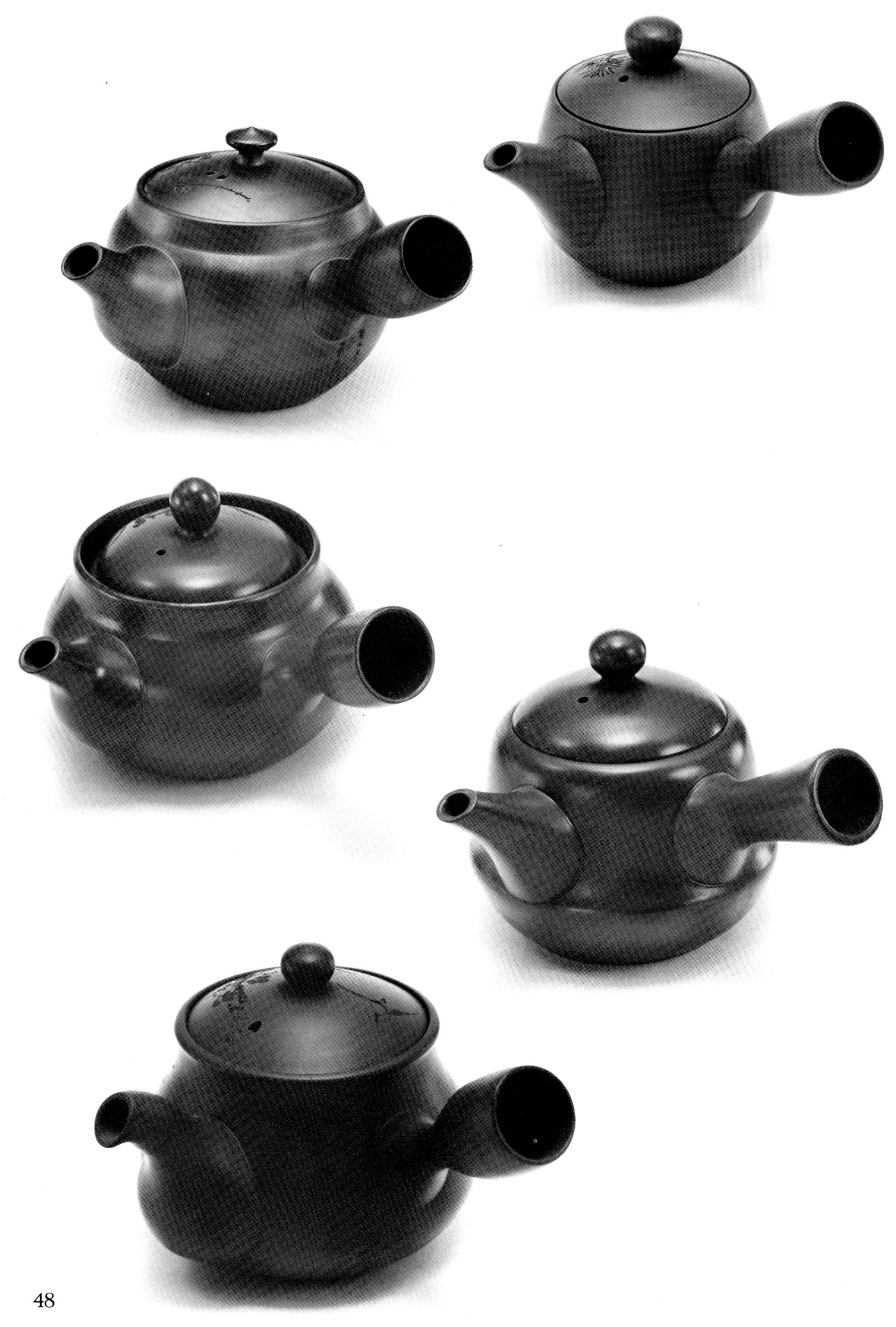

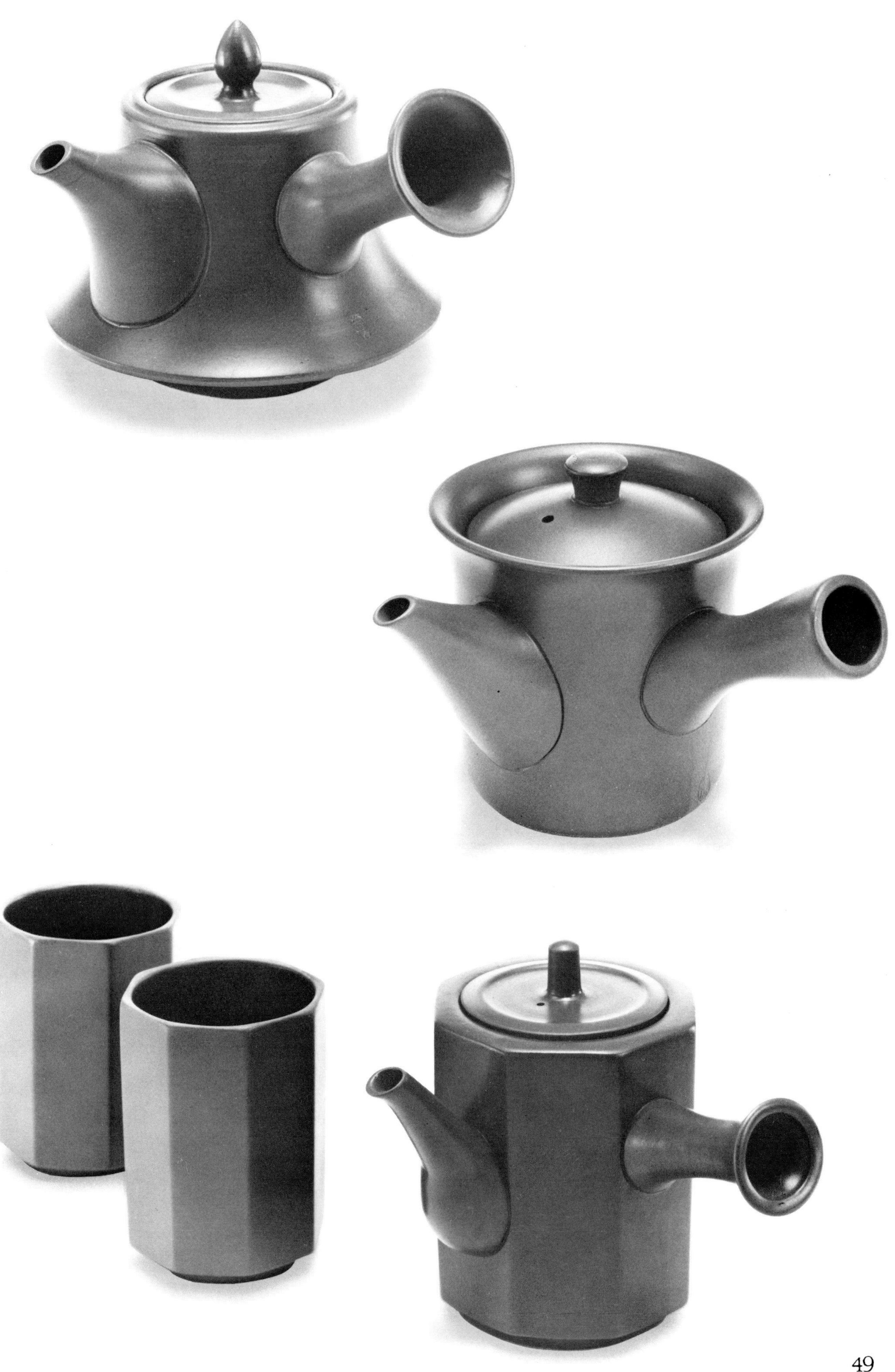

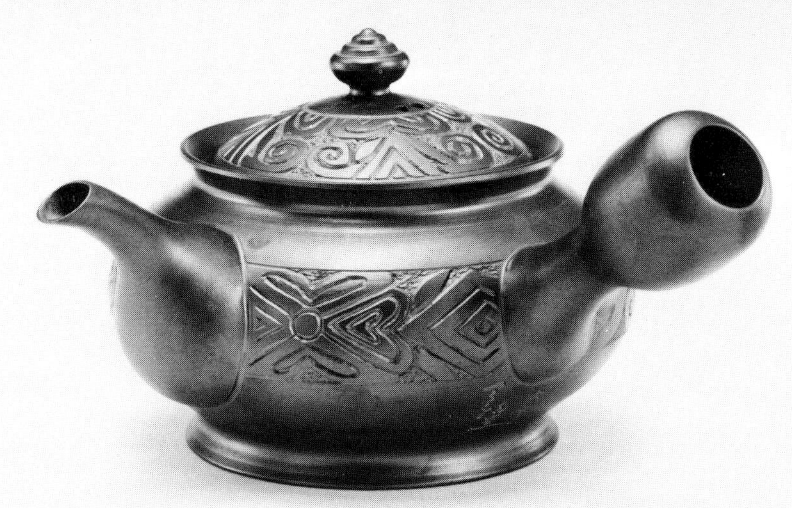

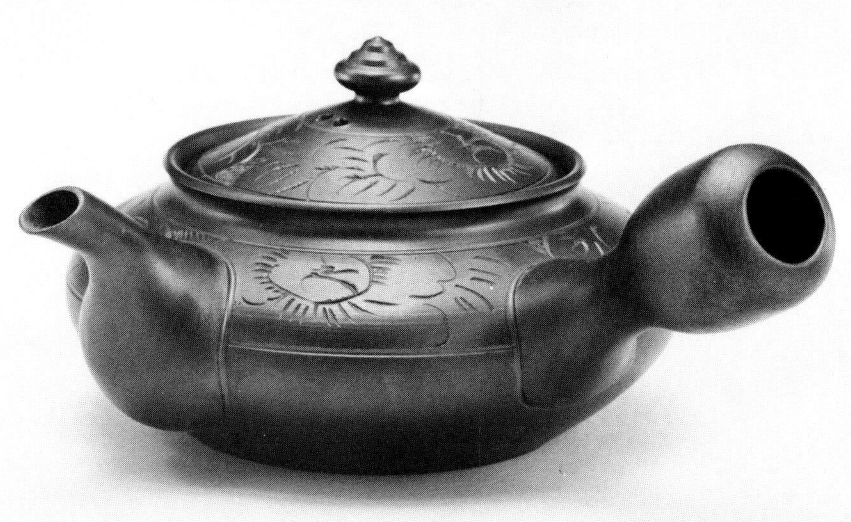

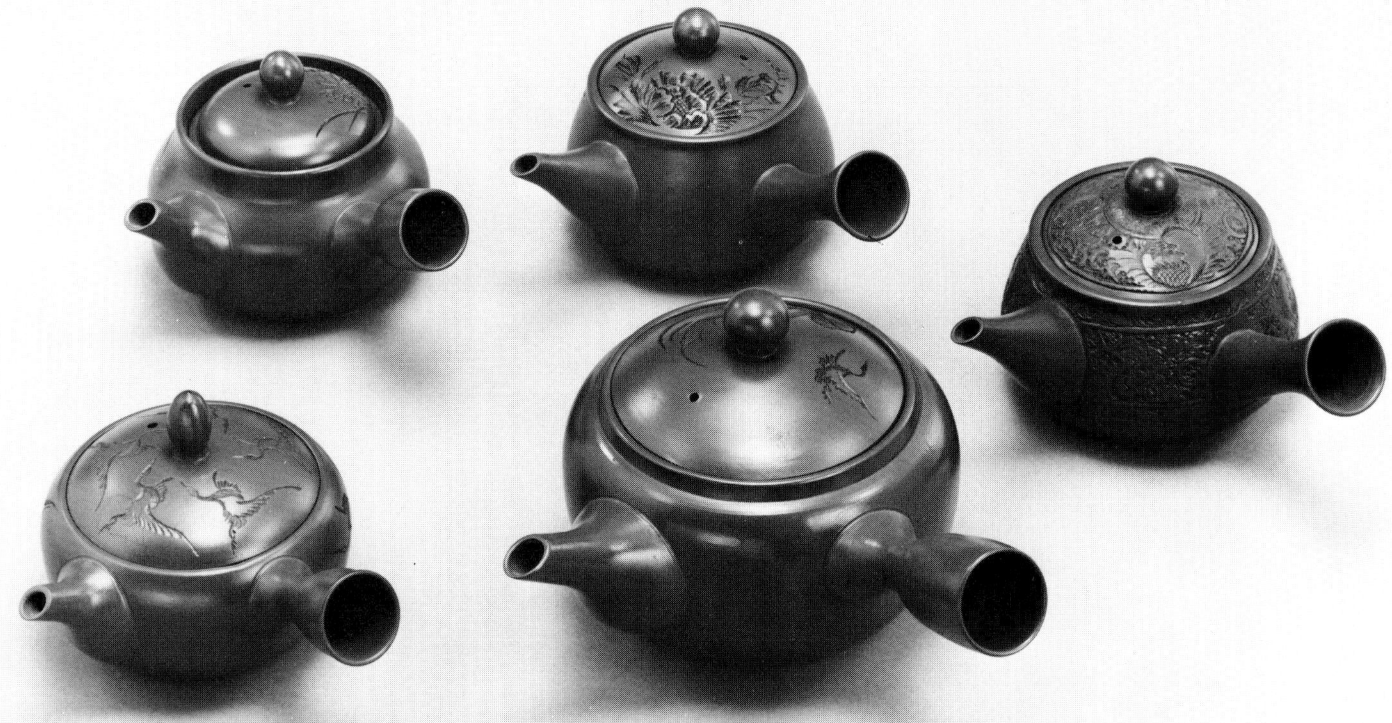

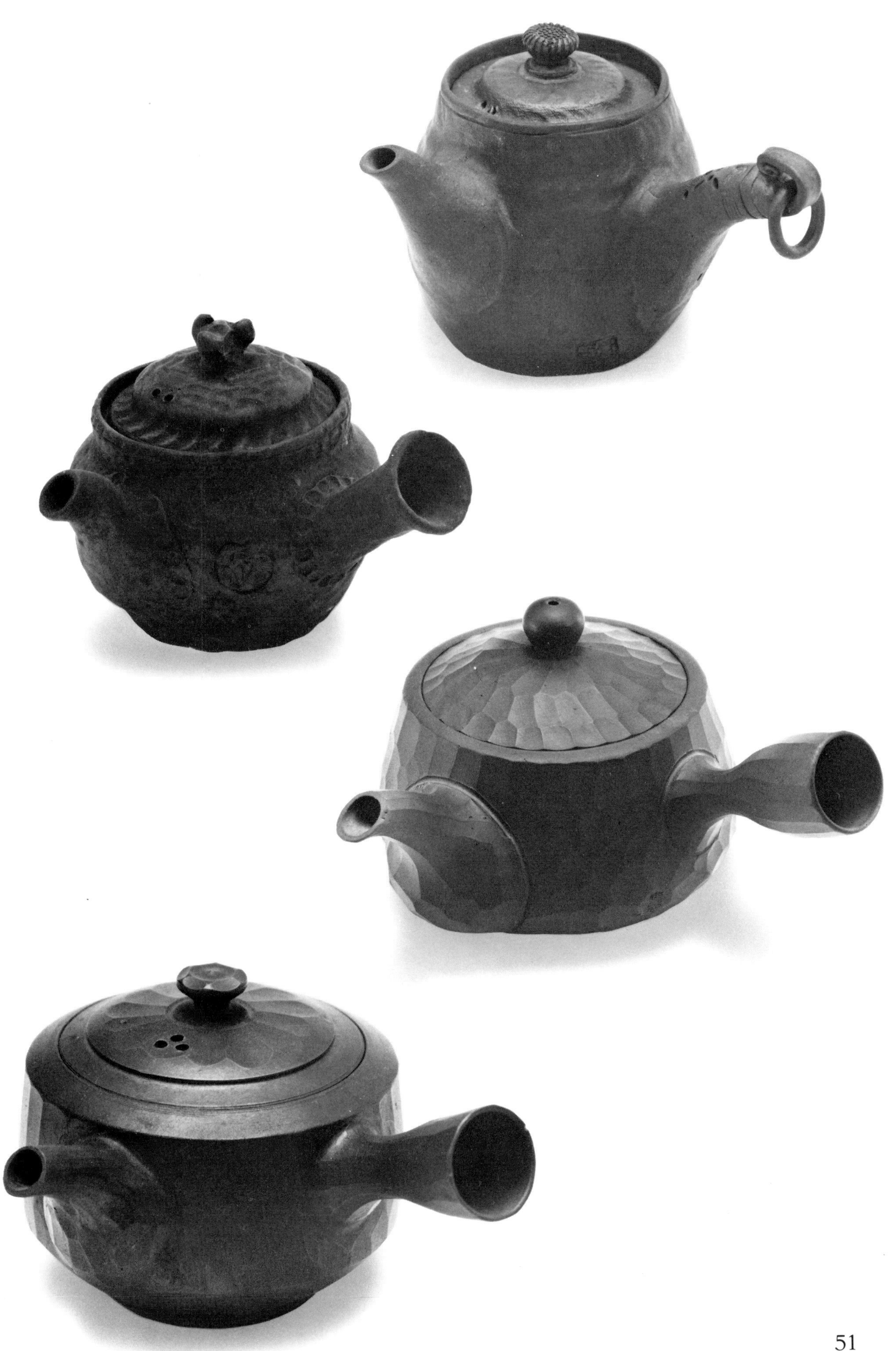

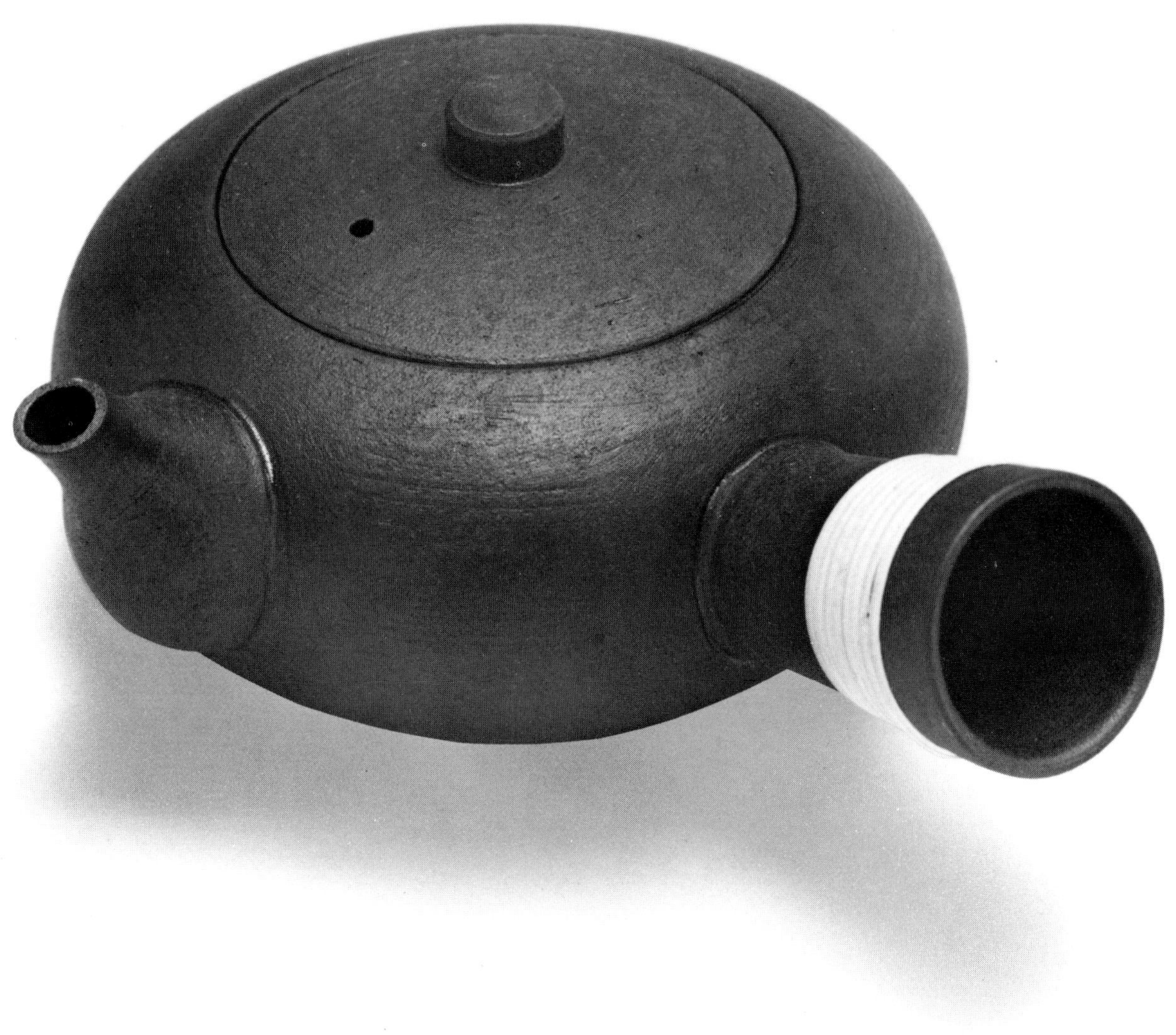

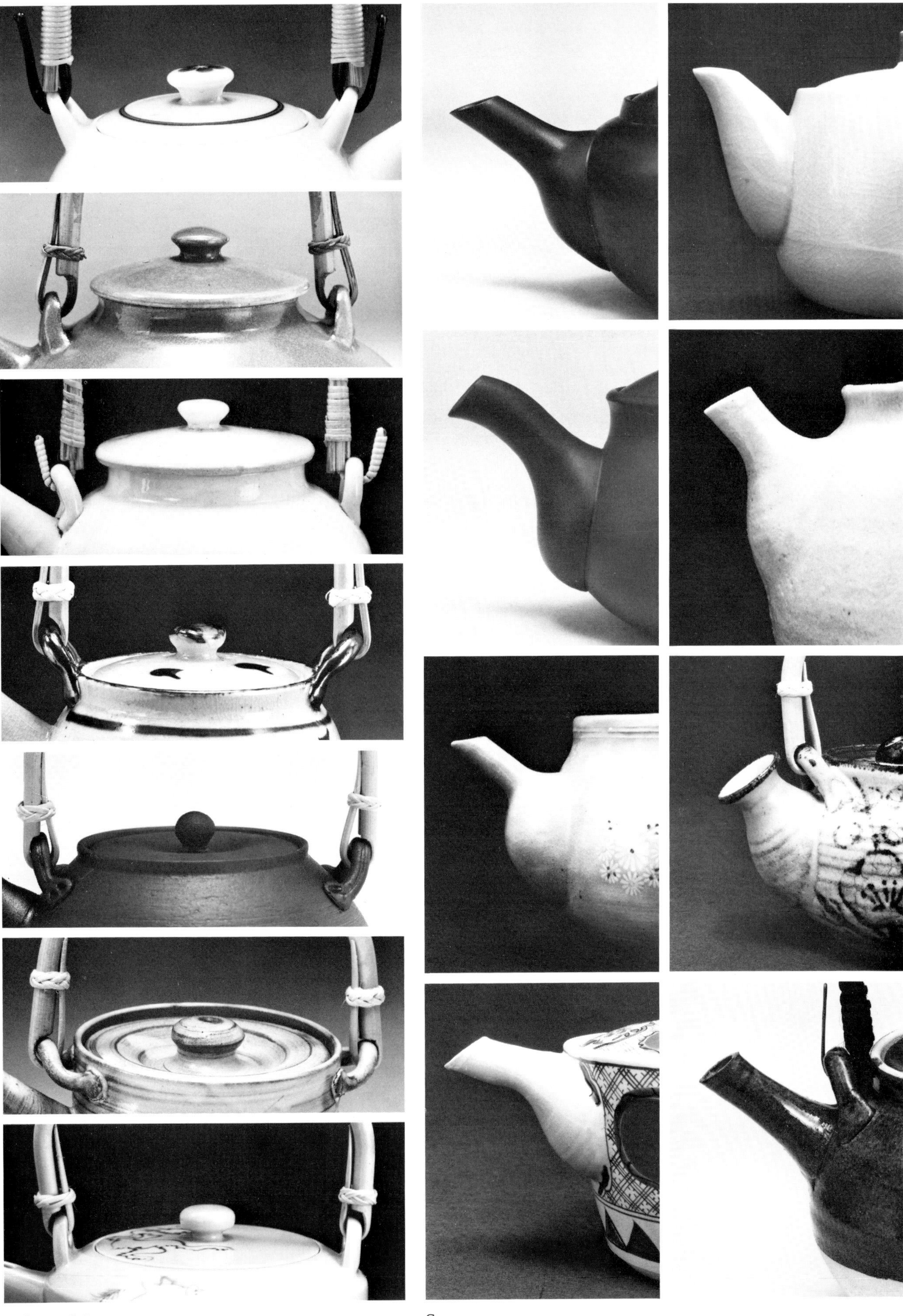

Lids and Lugs

Spouts

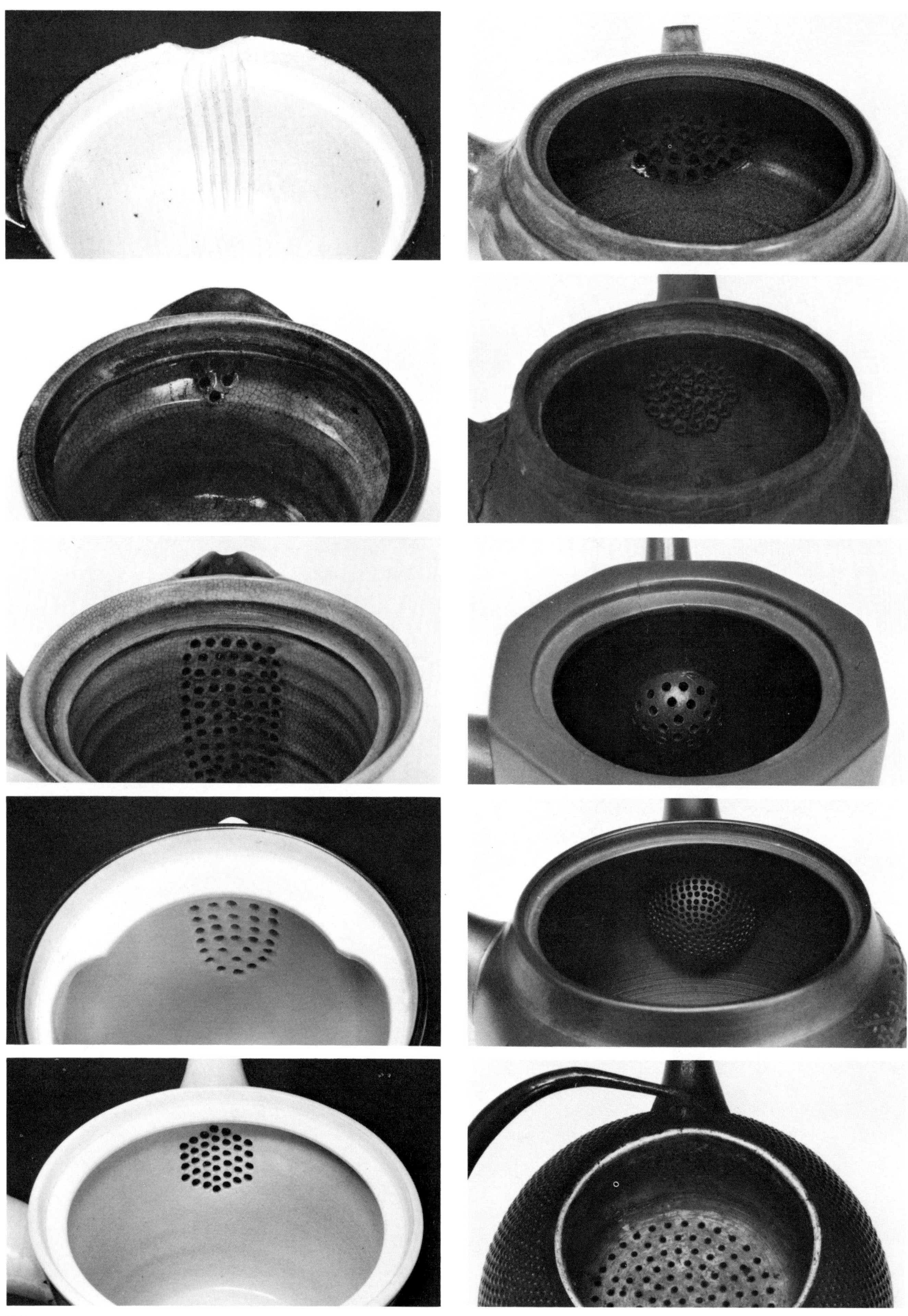

"Strainers"

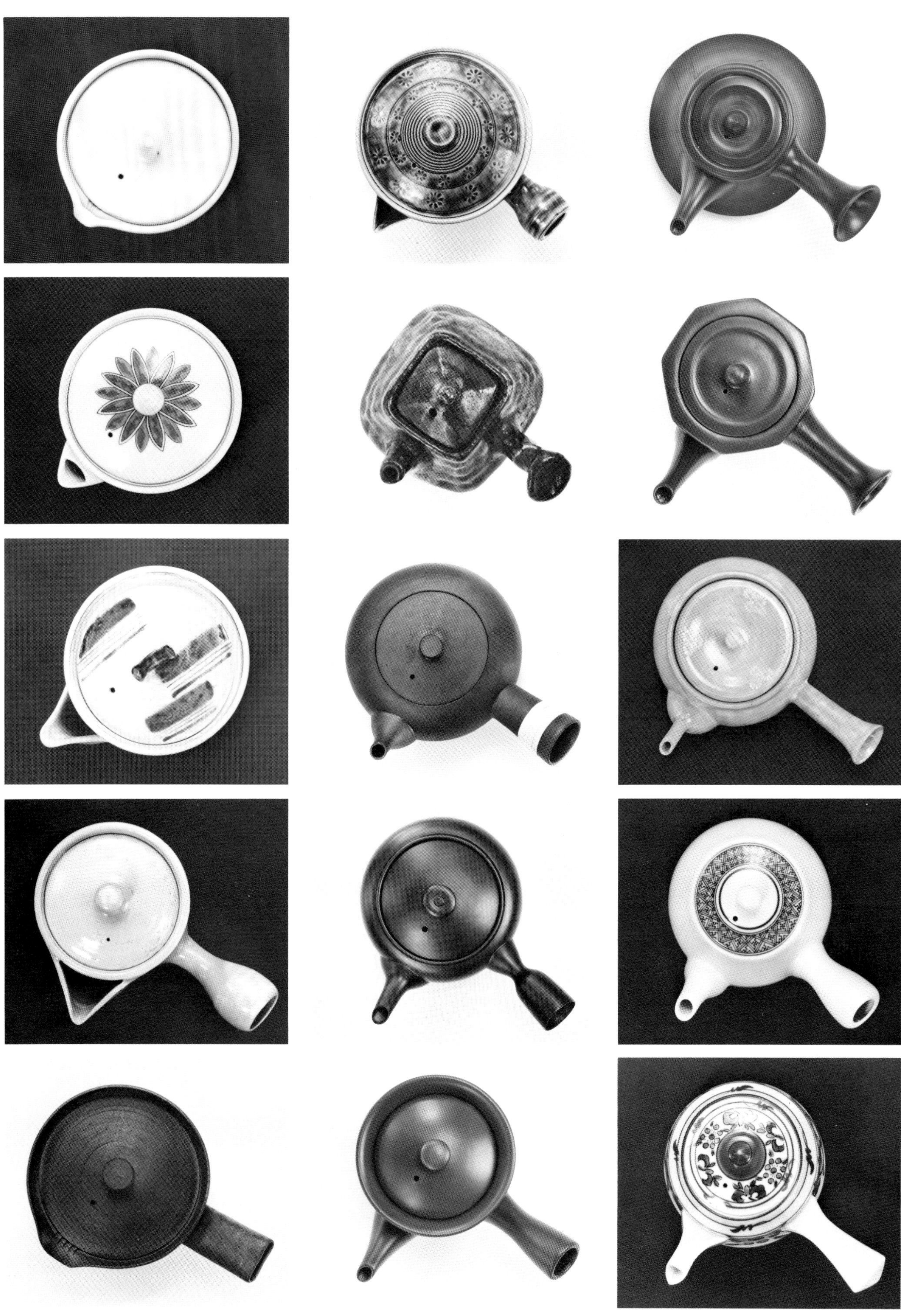

Kyusu Spouts and Handles

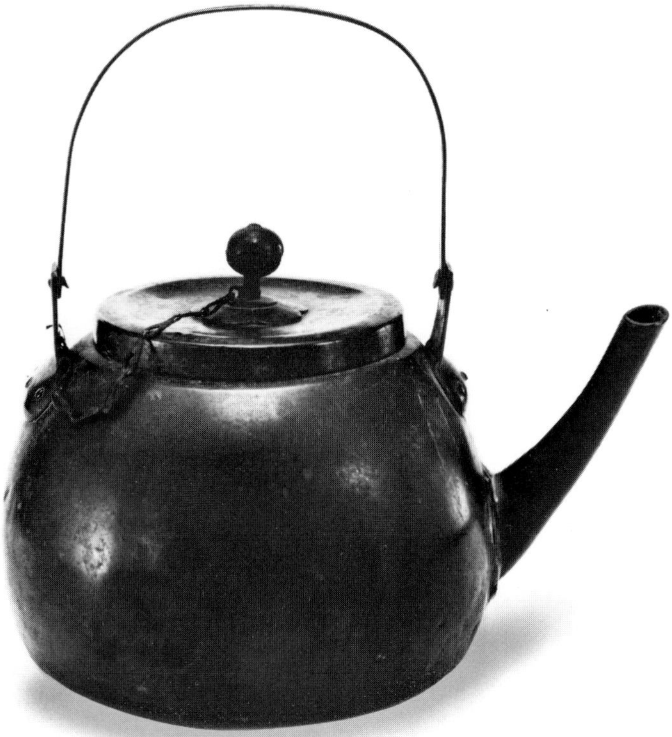

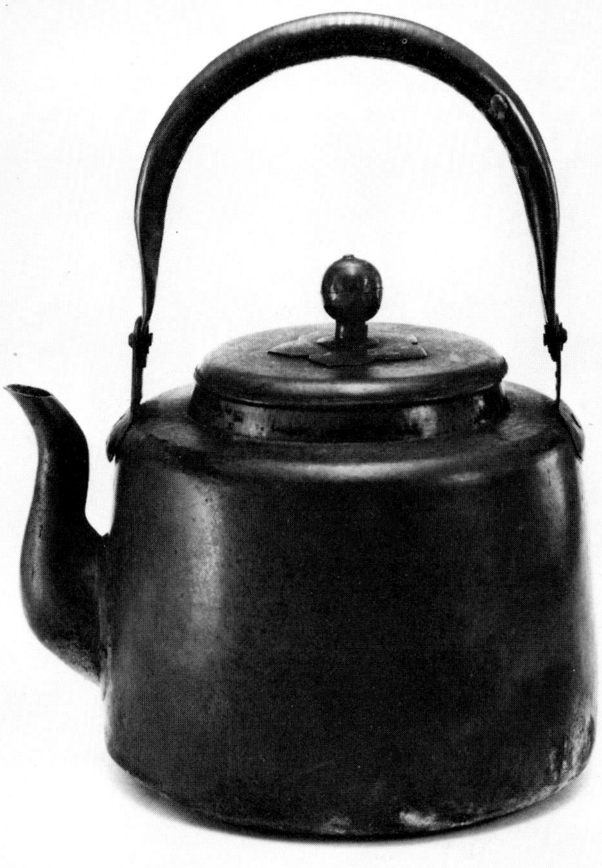

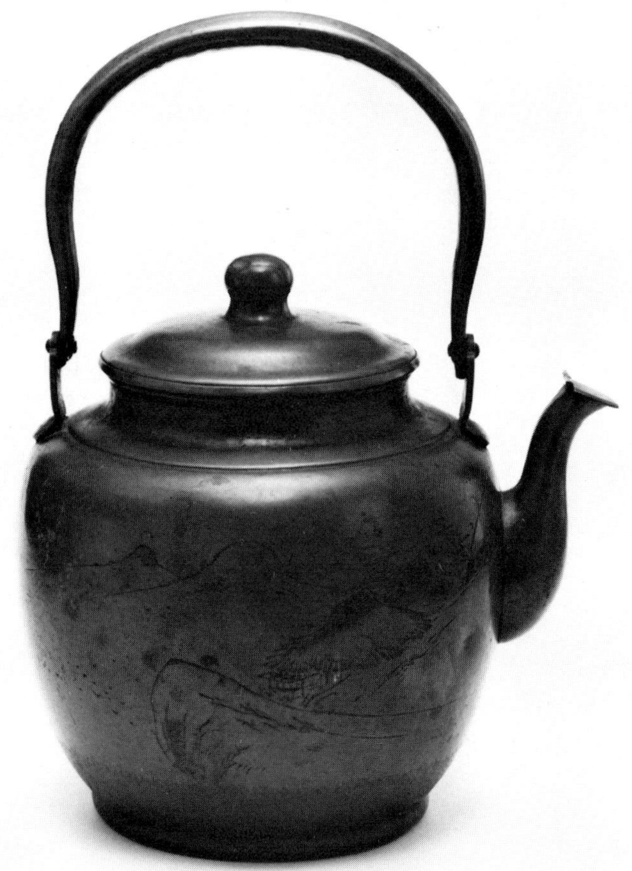

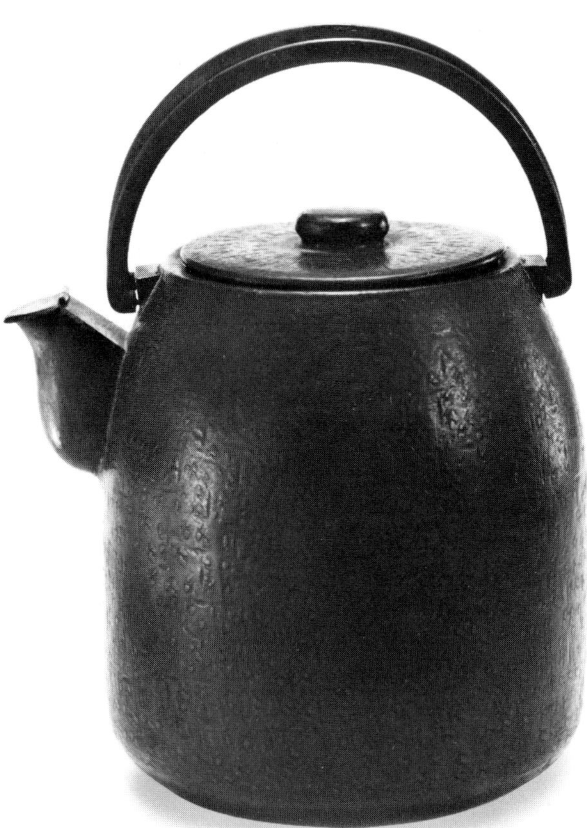

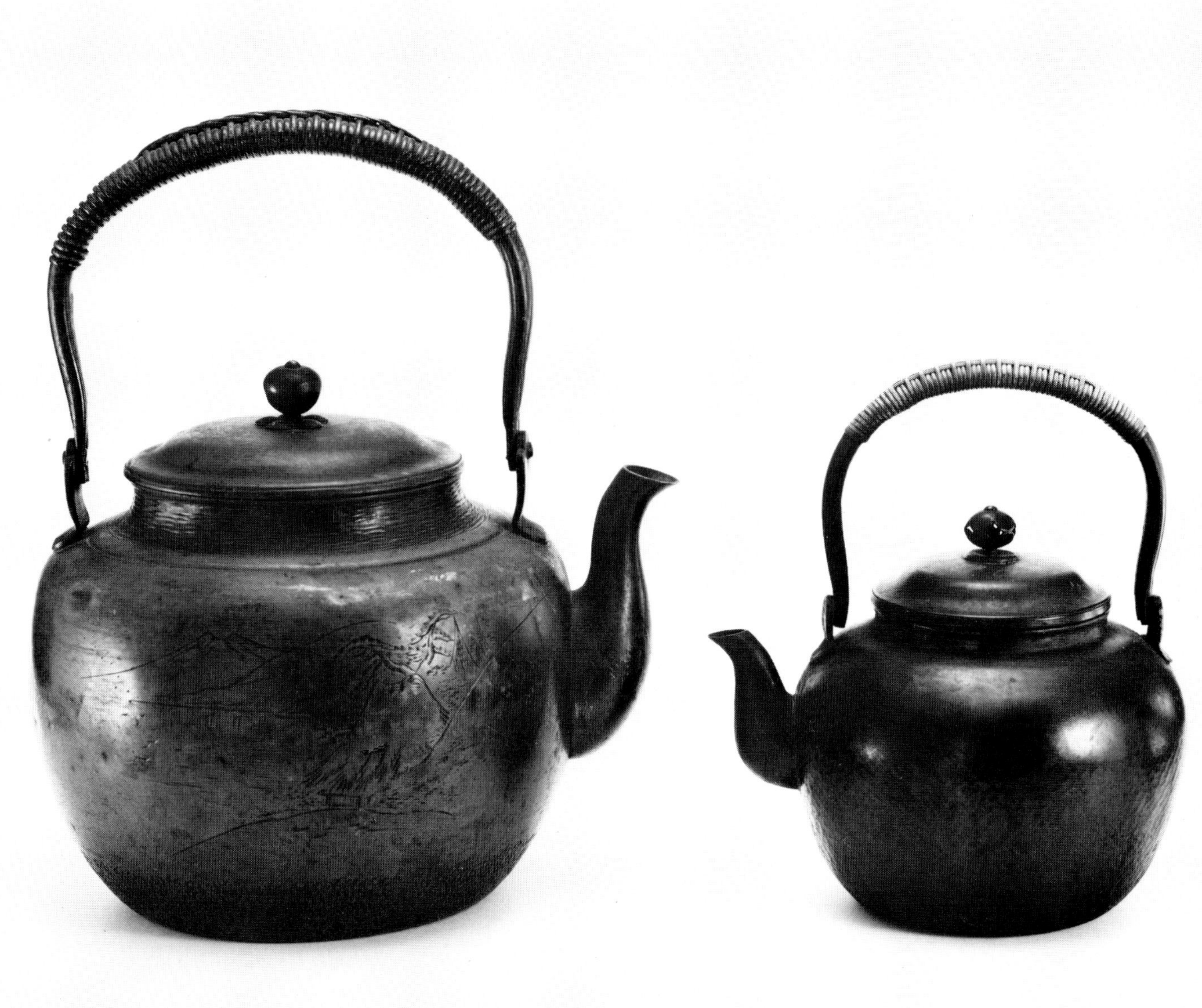

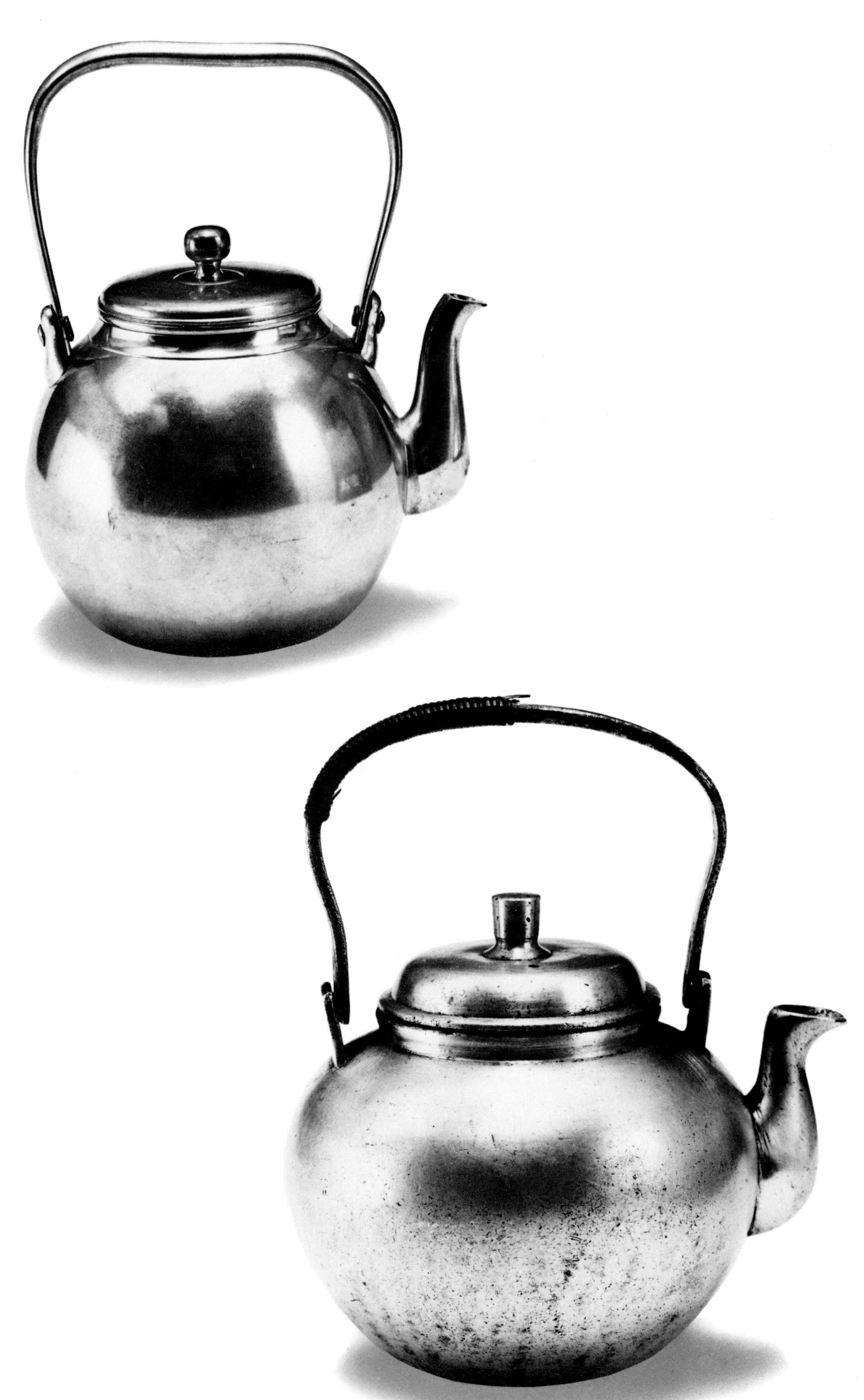

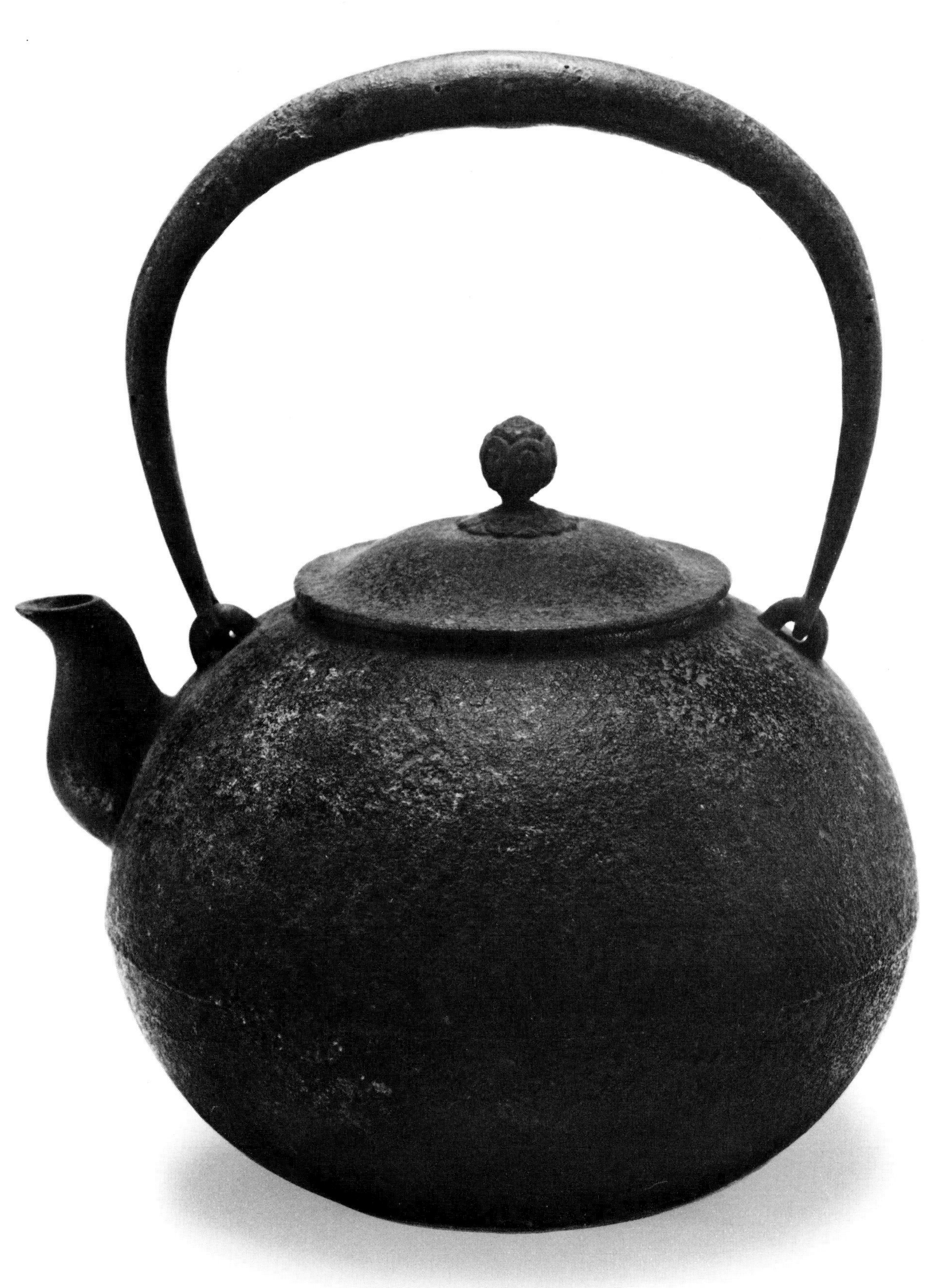

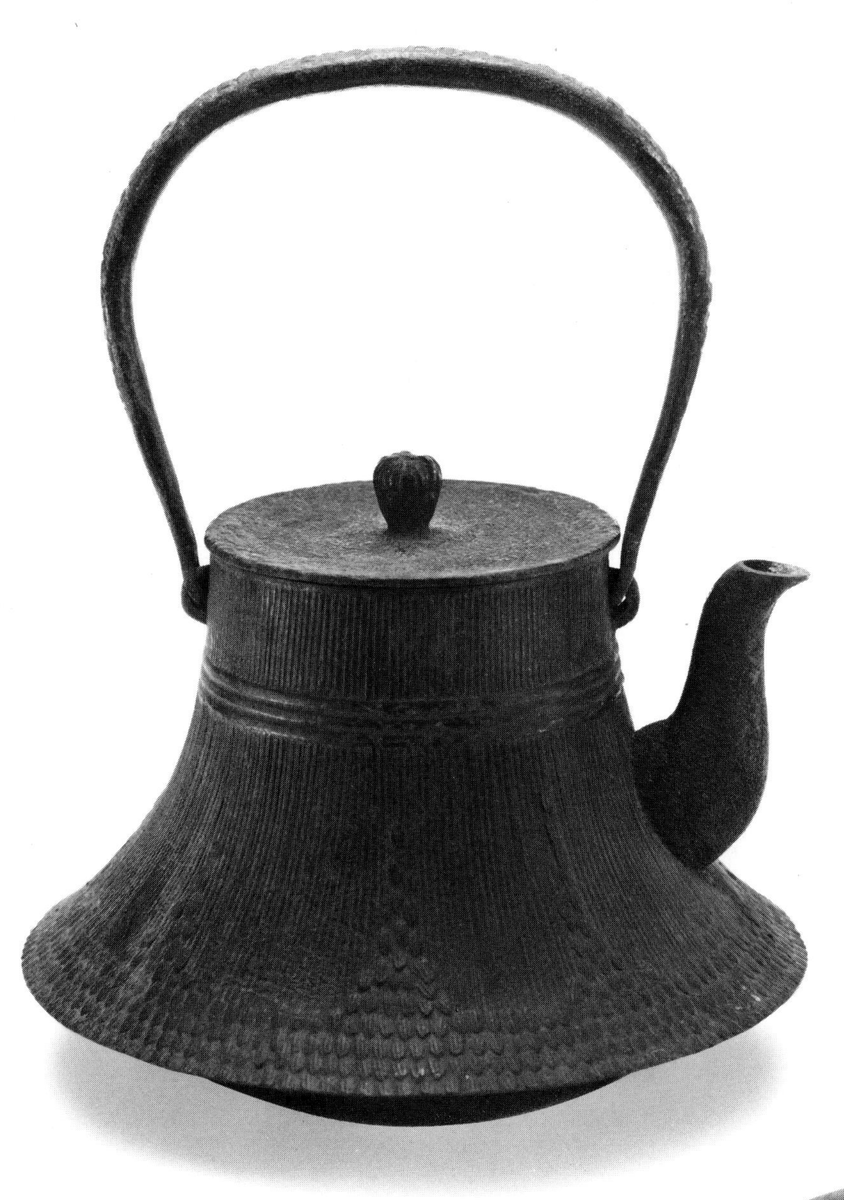

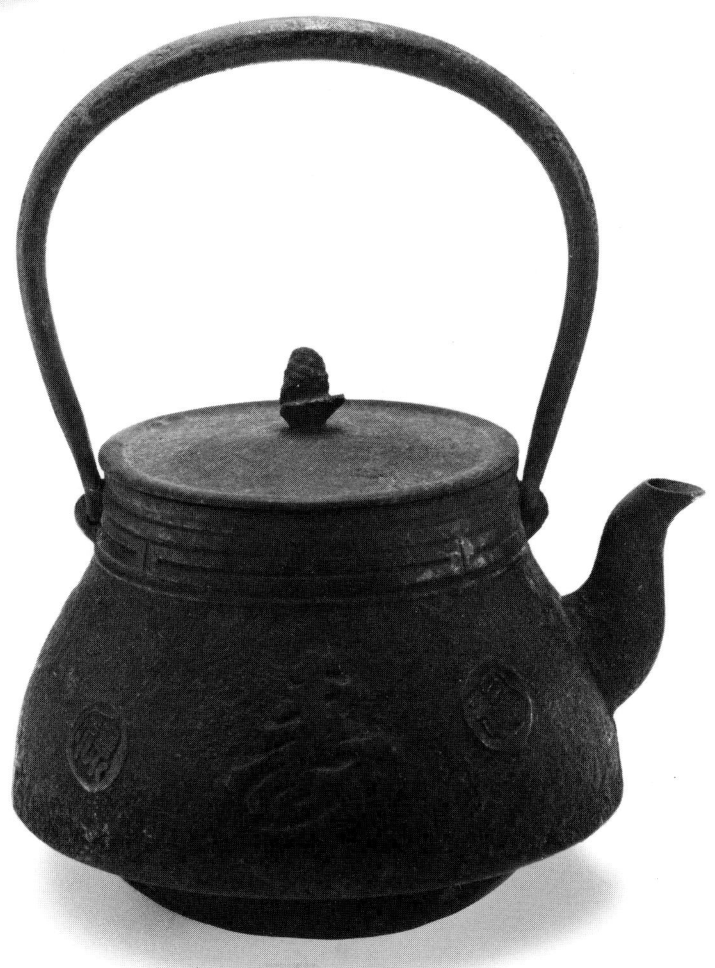

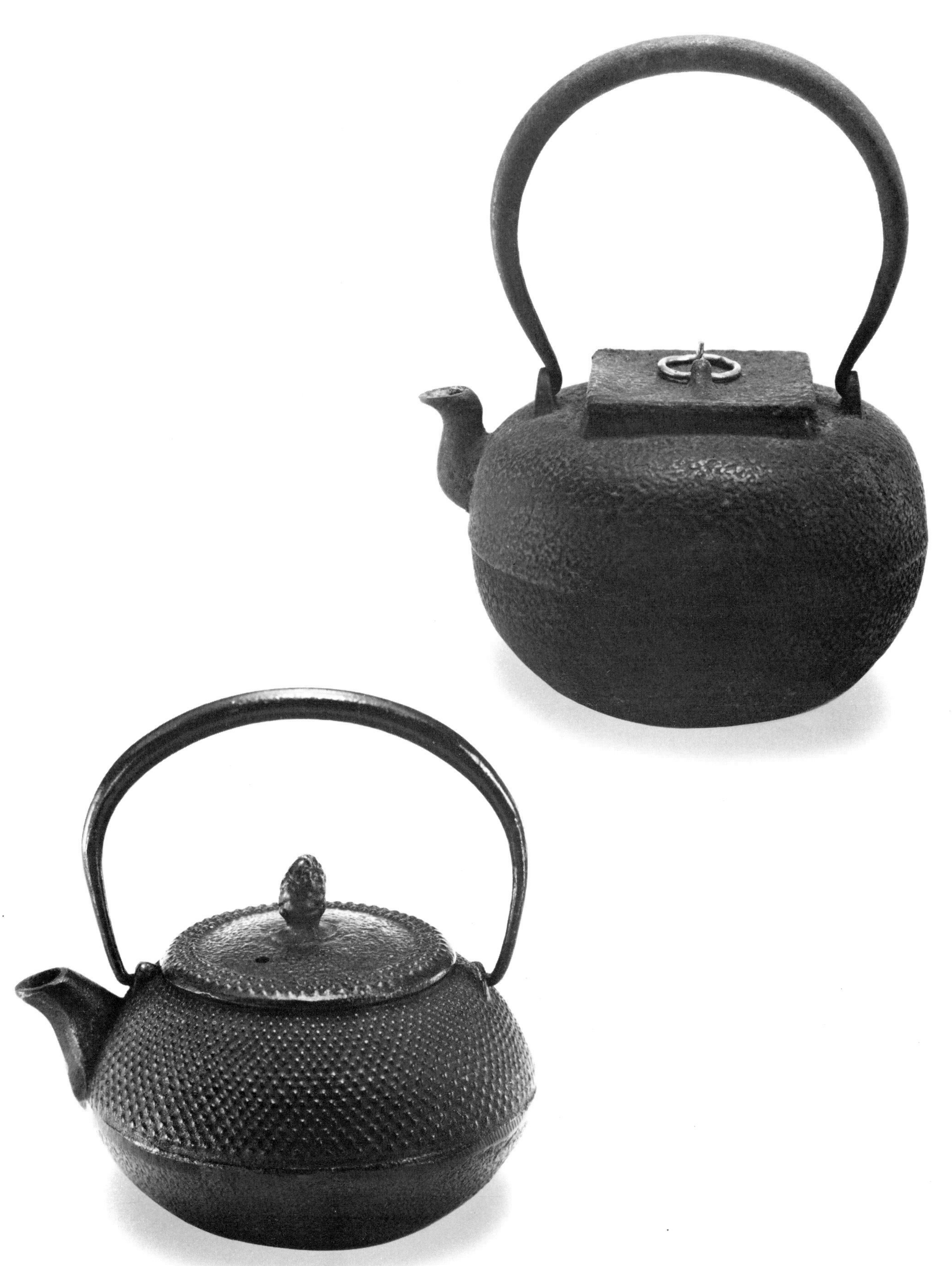

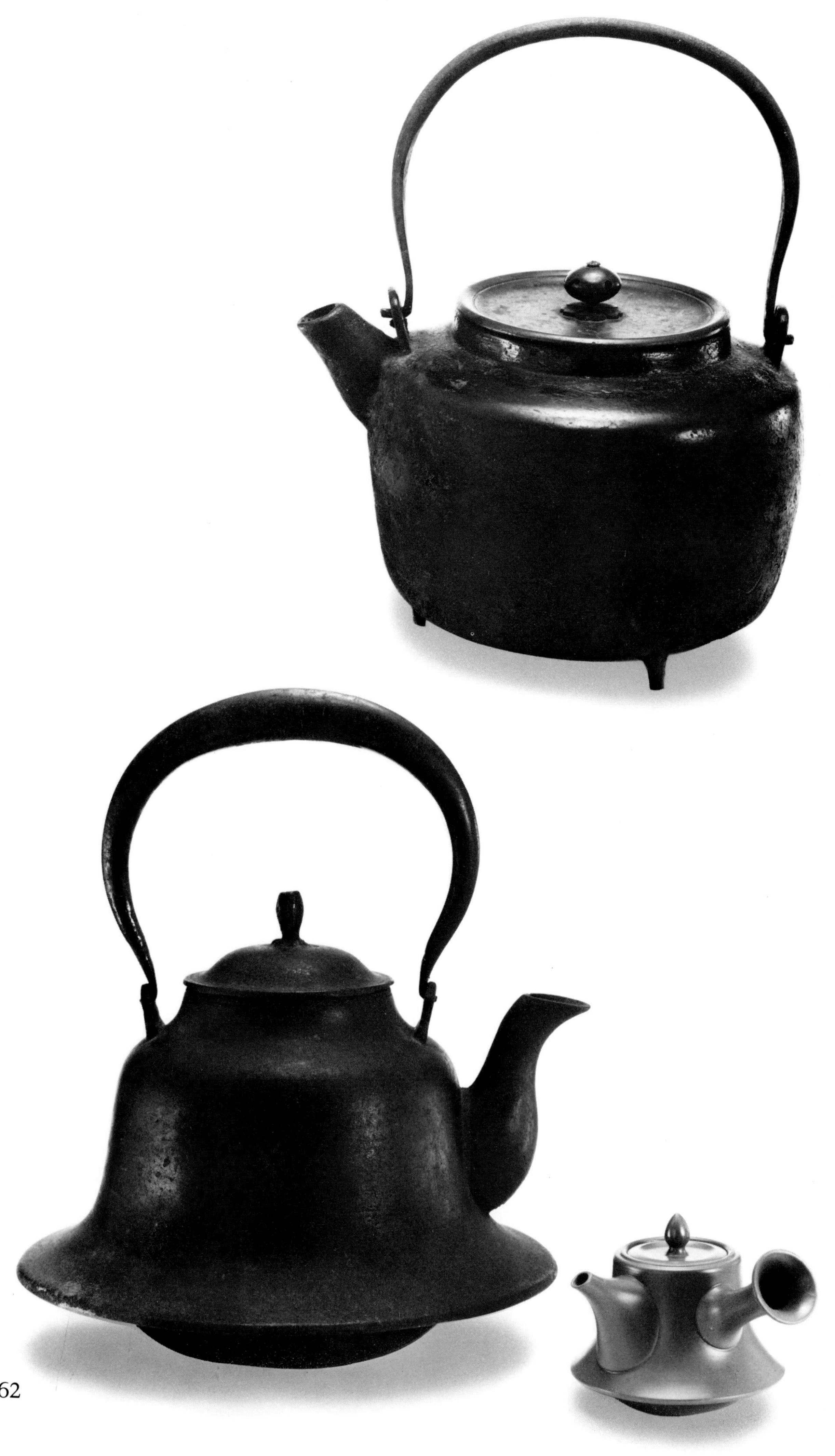

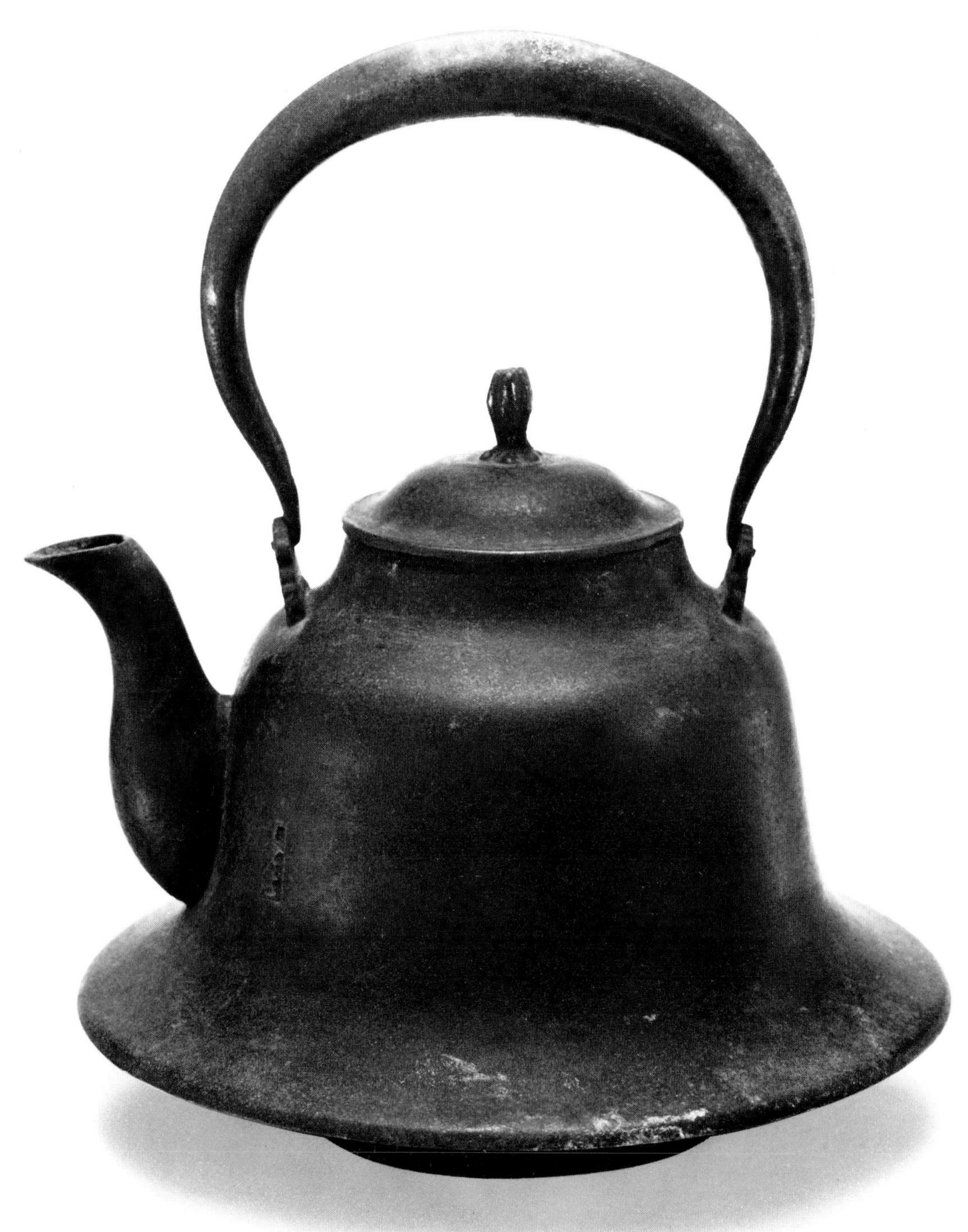

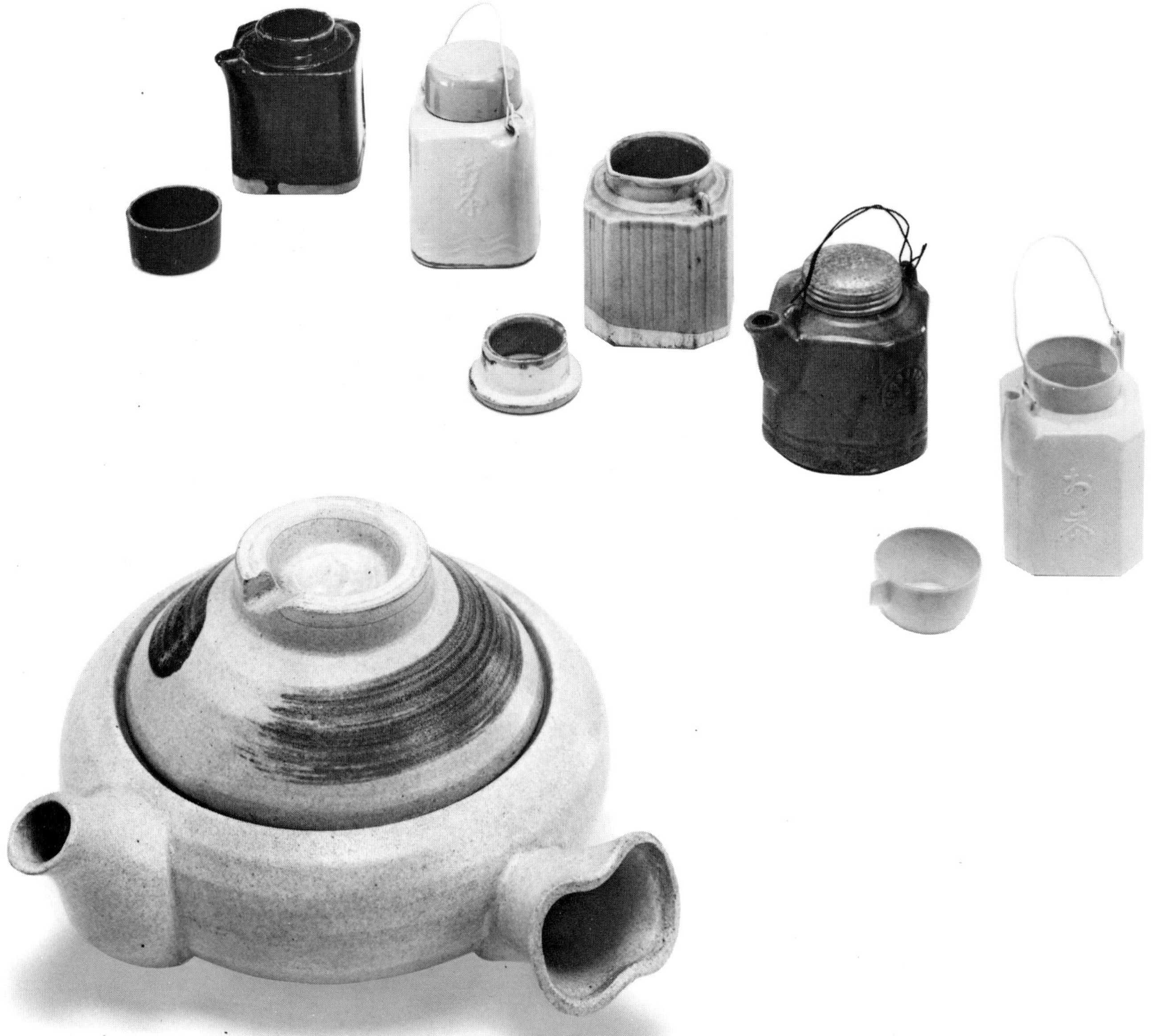

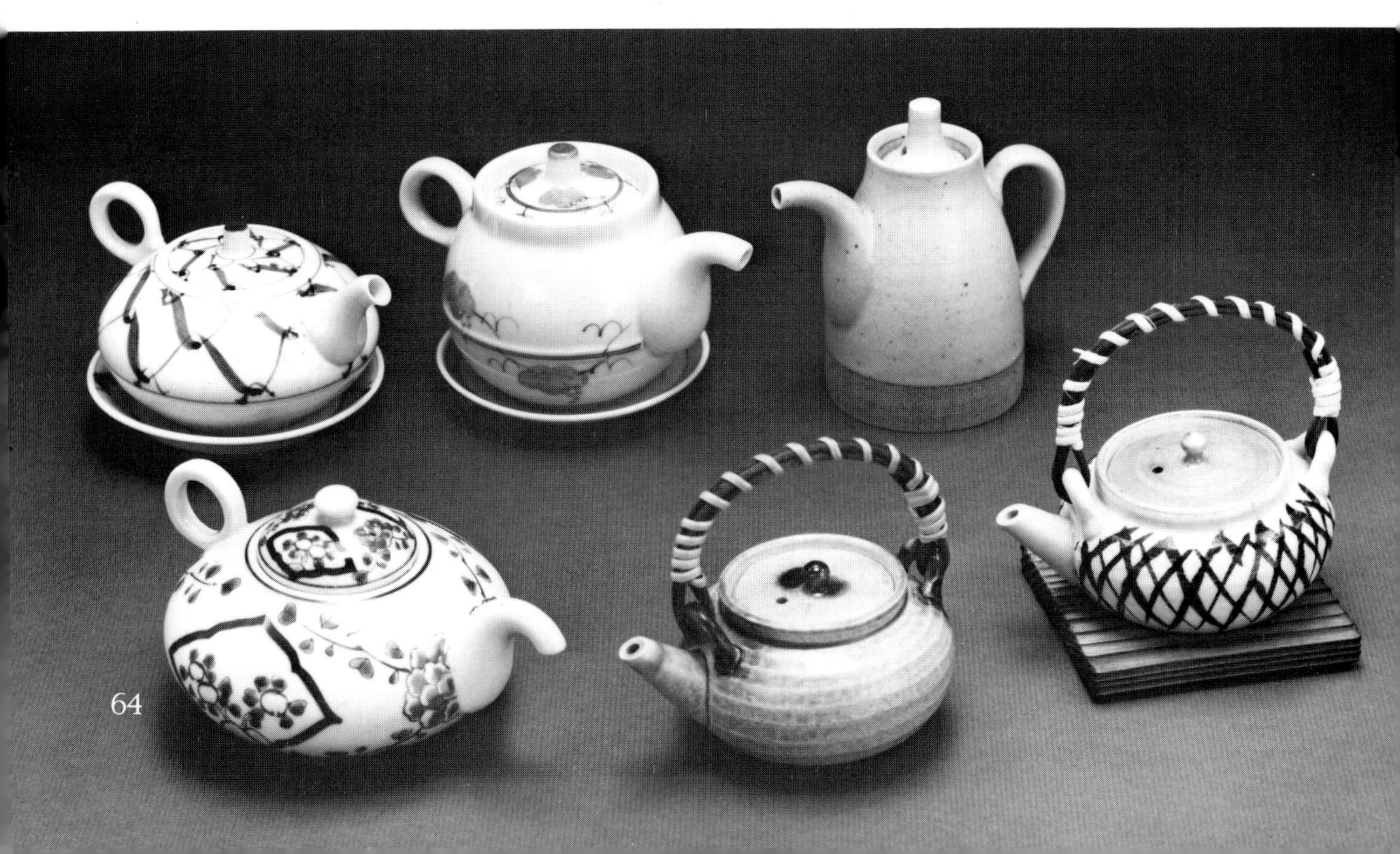

The Making of a Teapot

Body

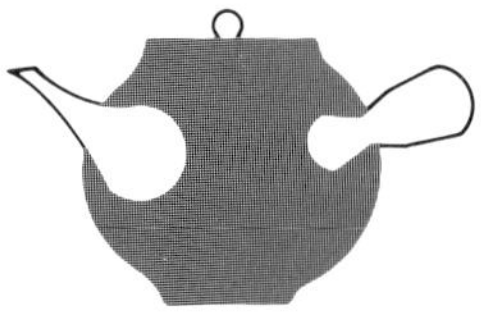

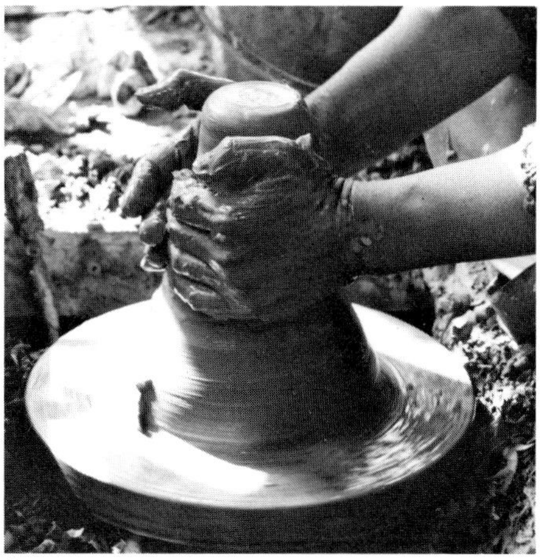

1

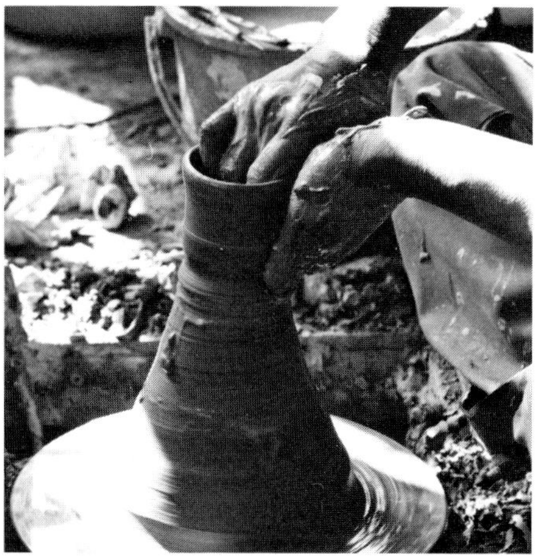

2

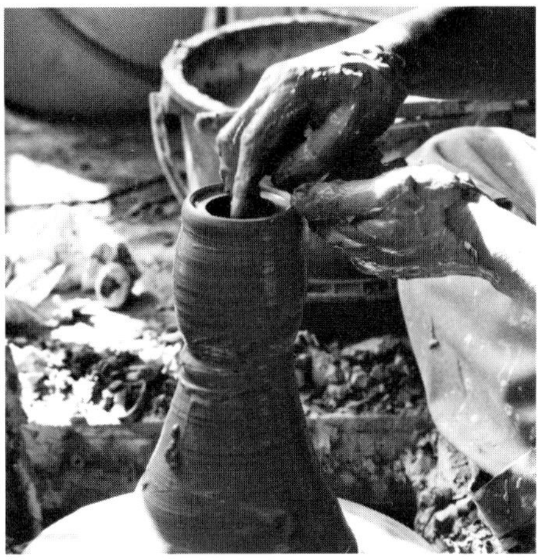

3

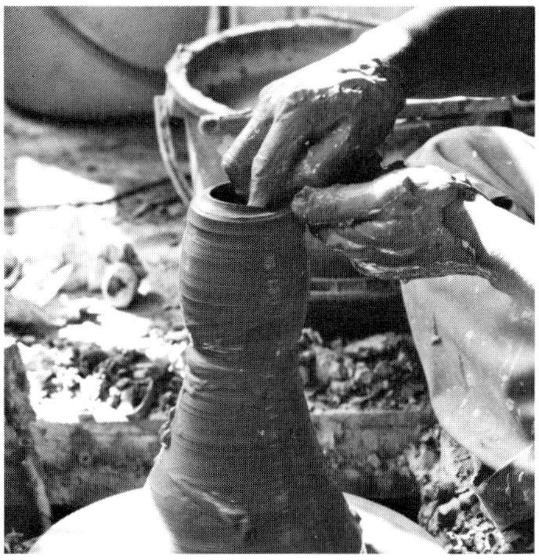

4

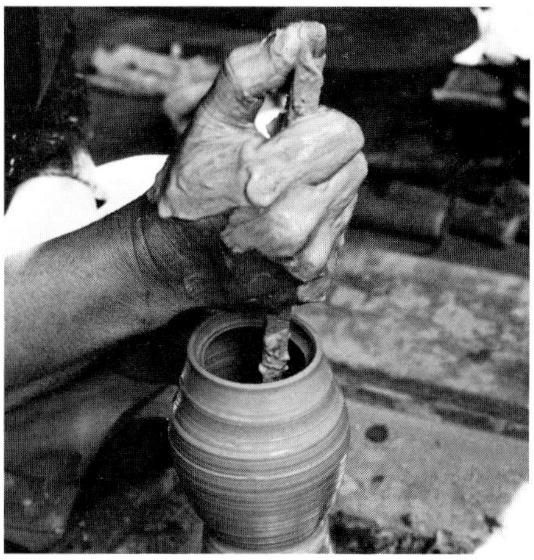

5

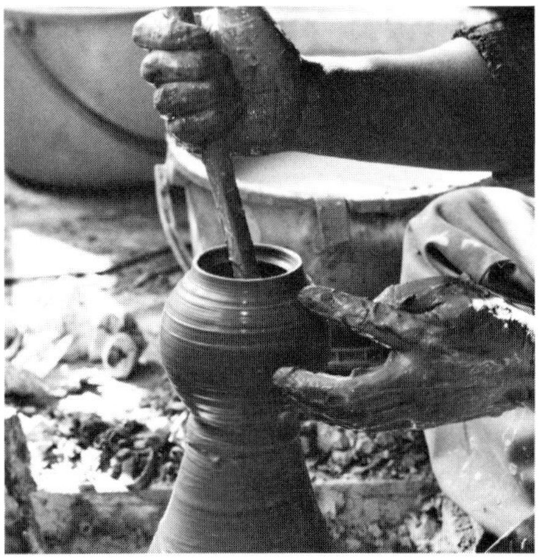

6

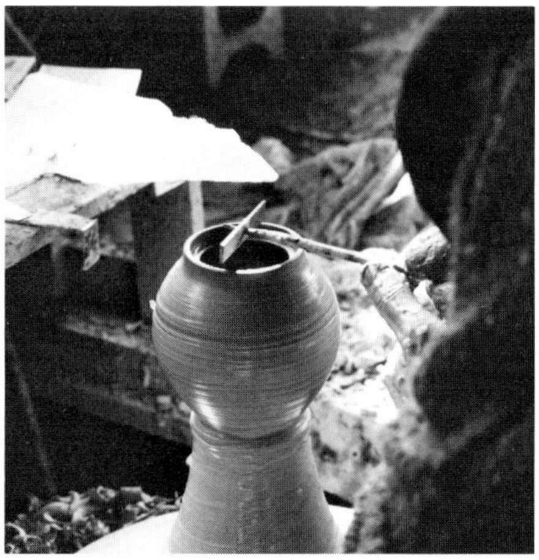

7

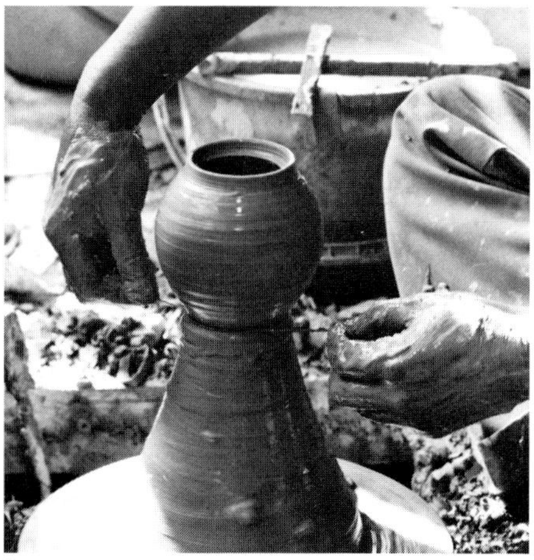

8

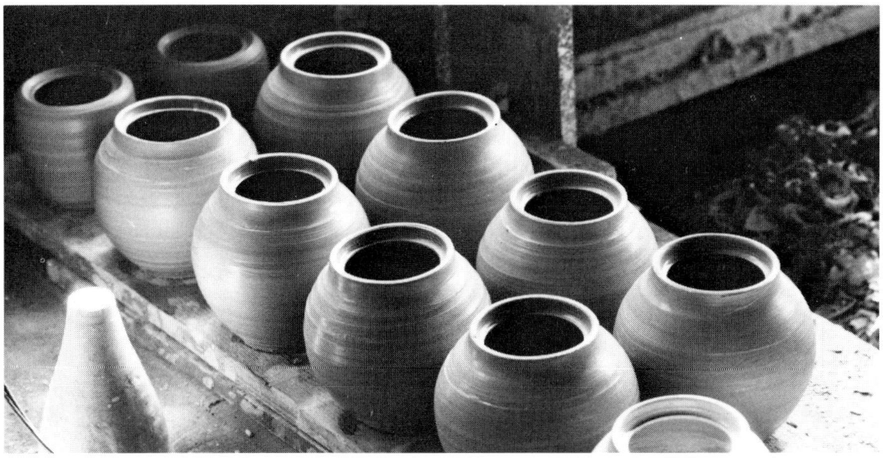

9

Lid

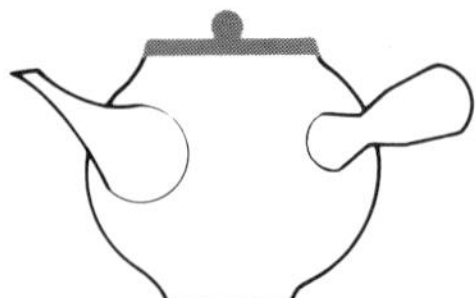

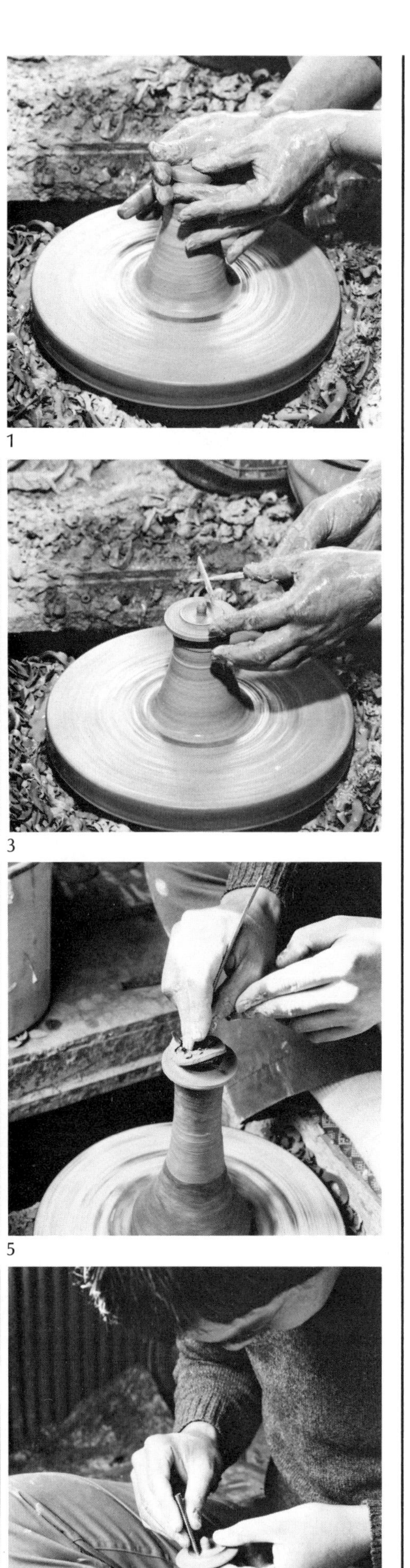

1

2

3

4

5

6

7

Spout

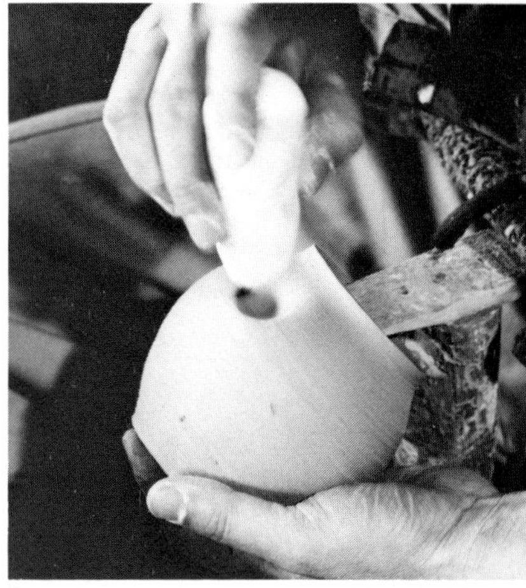

4

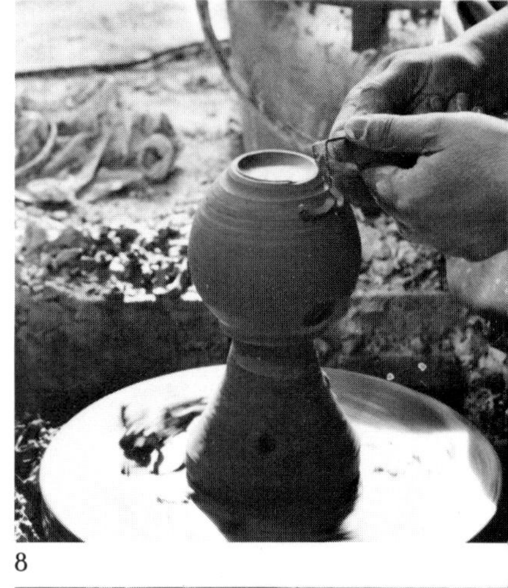

8

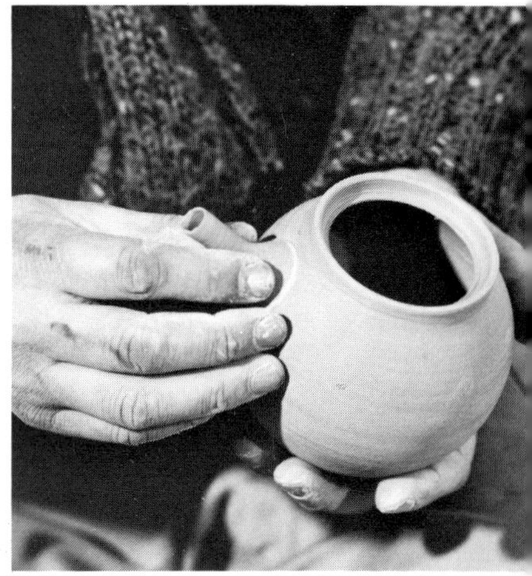

12

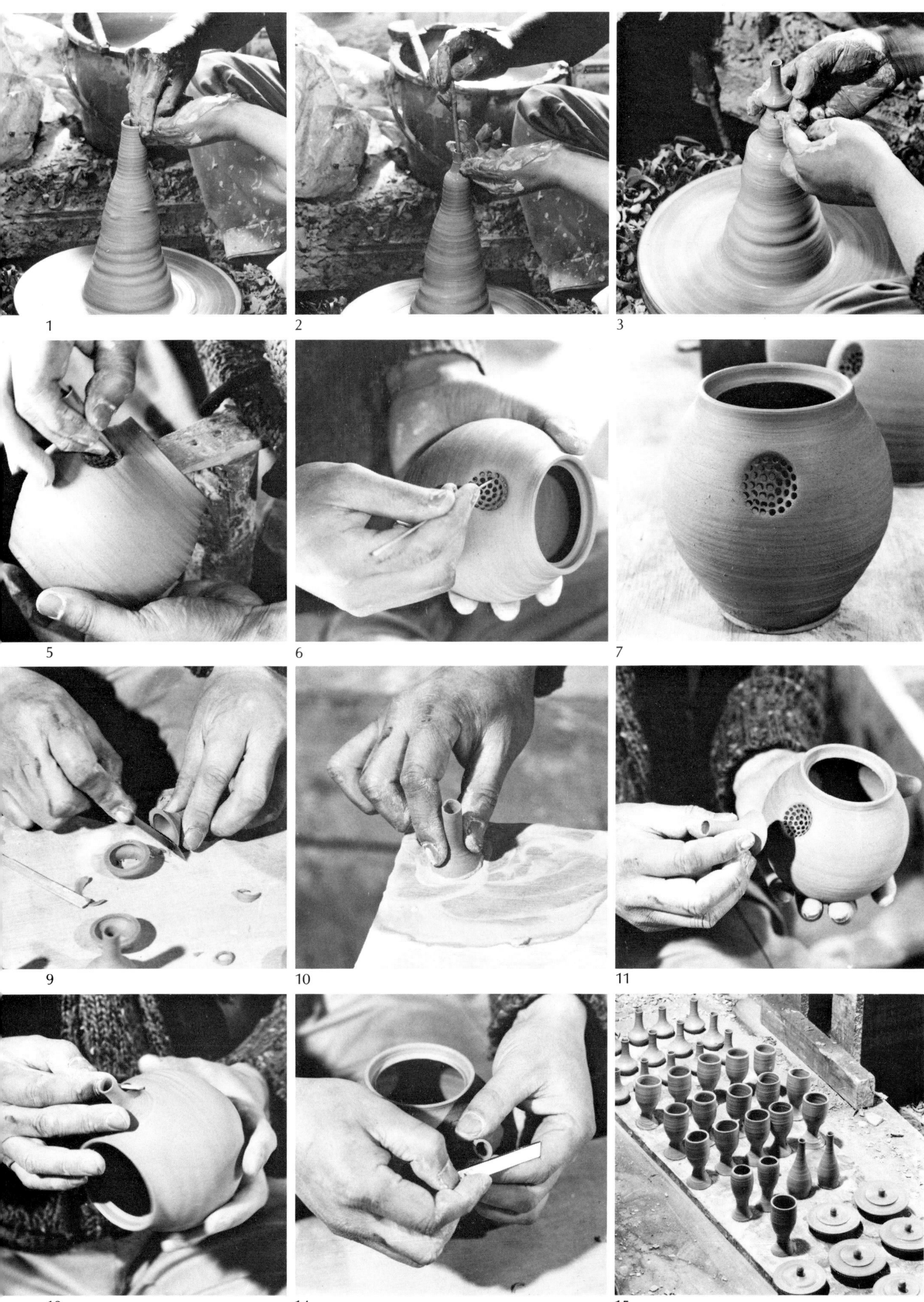
1 2 3
5 6 7
9 10 11
13 14 15

Handle

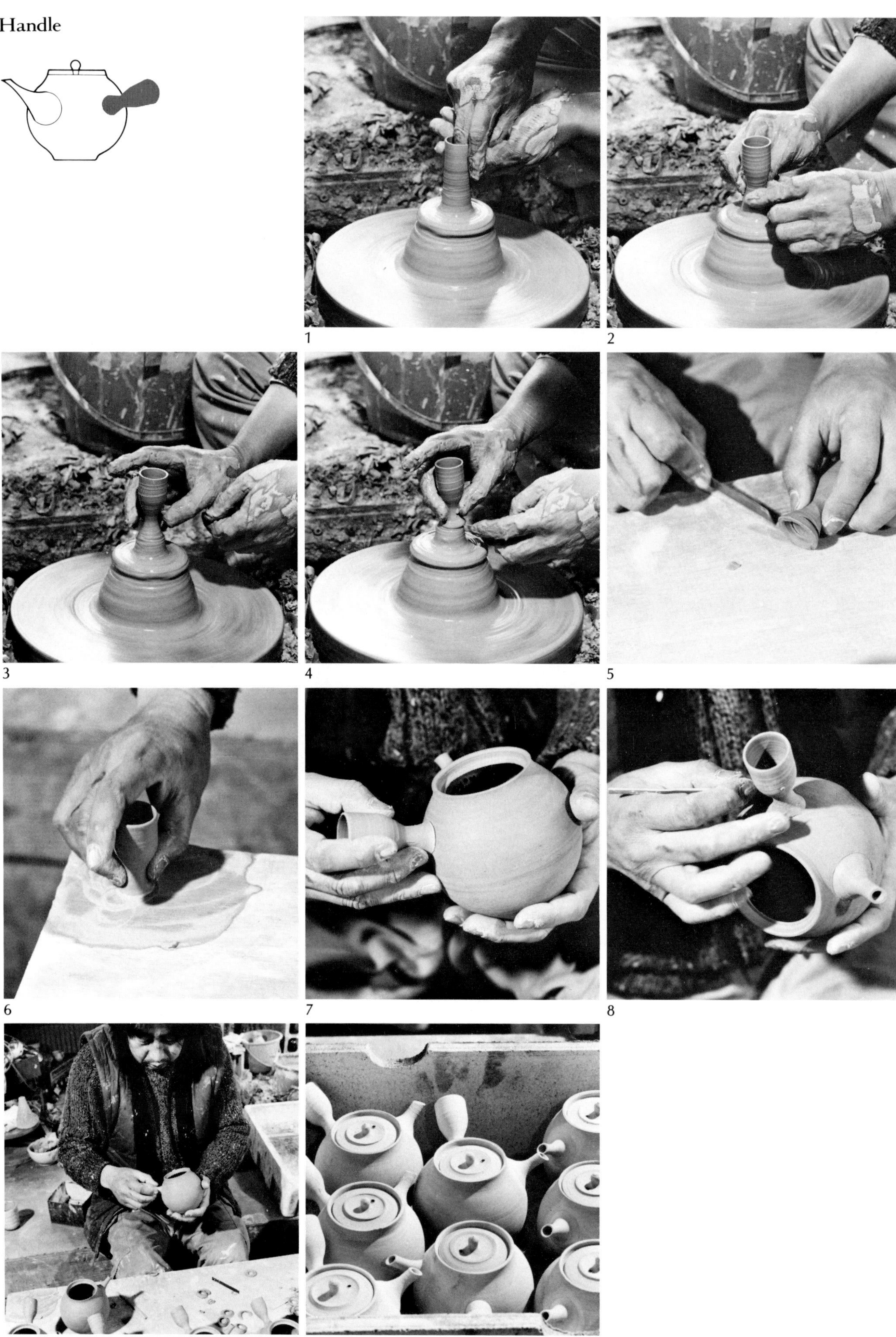

The Photographs

The first group of teapots (pages 9–13) pictured here are often identified in Japan as "medicine teapots" (*kusuri dobin*). One of the original uses of these pots was to brew infusions of herbal medicines. They were also used simply as kettles to heat water, and for this reason will be referred to here as kettle teapots. Today their most common use is the ordinary one of steeping and serving tea.

The major characteristic of these kettle teapots is that they can be used directly on an open flame. To allow this, they are unglazed on the bottom and are made of porous, refractory clay. Stoneware and porcelain, the conventional materials for teapots, cannot be used directly over a flame without breakage. This is because porcelain and stoneware clays fire at high temperatures and become vitrified. Such clay bodies transmit heat efficiently, so that if the pot body varies in thickness, or even if the glaze thickness varies, the resulting uneven transmission of heat will cause the pot to break. With a porous, refractory clay, heat is transmitted gently and evenly, which minimizes breakage. For the same reason, the surface in contact with the flame must be unglazed.

Most of the kettle teapots today are high fired, but the original kettle teapot was low-fired earthenware. Because this material can be used directly on an open flame, various cooking utensils of unglazed earthenware were widely used in the traditional Japanese kitchen. Some, in fact, have great antiquity, and have not changed significantly in shape or function since neolithic or protohistoric times, but today most of these objects have gone out of use or have been transformed into glazed, decorative vessels, following changes in life-style, eating habits, and tastes.

The spout of kettle teapots is usually straight and narrow. This is the most primitive type of spout; the same spout type is found on late neolithic (late Jōmon period) pots in Japan. Liquid gushes out of such a spout, and the flow is hard to control. Curved spout designs allow the liquid to be poured more easily and with more control.

In western Japan, which is considered the best country for the type of highly esteemed wild mushroom known as *matsutake*, kettle teapots are carried along on mushroom-gathering outings in autumn. The fresh *matsutake* mushrooms are put into the pot without adding any liquid, and the pot is placed over a fire. In this way the mushrooms are cooked by steaming them in their own juices. Today this mushroom cookery has been adapted by fancy and expensive restaurants—served in chickly "rustic" vessels and gussied up with other ingredients—but originally it was simply a rural enjoyment, using the kettle teapot.

Kettle teapots are made in large numbers at Shigasaki (pages 9; 12, top left), Mashiko (page 12, bottom left), and at numerous local kilns throughout the country. A few kilns still produce a limited number of the older, low-fired earthenware type of kettle teapot. A kiln specializing in this type of earthenware is Mimaya, near Takamatsu in Shikoku (pages 11, top; 12, bottom right). Ōhara in Okayama Prefecture, Shiraishi in Saga Prefecture, and Sano in Yamaguchi Prefecture also make earthenware teapots. Glaze on such earthenware pots is a relatively recent development; low-fired glazes are usually used, whereas the high-fired kettle pots are glazed with conventional stoneware glazes. Because the clay of these pots is quite porous, the inside is usually coated with a fine clay slip.

The second group of teapots, pictured on pages 14–17, is composed of those used for *bancha* tea. *Bancha* is inexpensive, everyday tea drunk after a Japanese meal. It is prepared in the same manner as Western black tea—boiling water is poured over leaves in the teapot. Most *bancha* teapots are stoneware or porcelain and are entirely glazed. A few are still made that can be used on a direct flame like a kettle teapot and that are, in fact, intermediate in the evolution of the modern *bancha* teapot from the ancestral earthenware kettle pot form.

A comparison of spouts on the *bancha* and kettle teapots shows the development from the primitive, straight spout to the curved spout that allows control and convenience in pouring (examples: pages 16, bottom; 17, top right and bottom left). Pots on page 18 display a flaring spout mouth. This is not just some designer's whimsy, but is a shape that aids in giving an even flow. The angle of the spout mouth is also important in allowing pouring control.

The origin of the Japanese word for teapot handle—*tsuru*—is not clear. One theory states that, since the pot was suspended from a pot-hanger over the hearth fire, the noun *tsuru* may have come from the verb "to suspend"—*tsurusu*. A second theory has it that handles were made of some kind of vine; the Japanese word for vine is *tsuru*. The latter theory seems the most direct and plausible at this time.

There are two types of teapot handles: one in which the handle material is bent inward through the lugs and one in which the material is bent outward (see pages 17, 30, 53). With the former, a ring is used to secure the handle and hold it in place; (usually) no ring is used with the outward-bending type. This latter type without ring utilizes metal wire or a metal strip, either bare or as a core around which other materials are wrapped. The metal acts as a spring and gives enough tension to keep the handle in an upright position. There are some exceptions, in which the outward-bending handle is of the conventional ring-secured type, without metal.

When pouring tea, the handle is held in one hand, and the lid is held down by the fingertips of the other hand (see sketch).

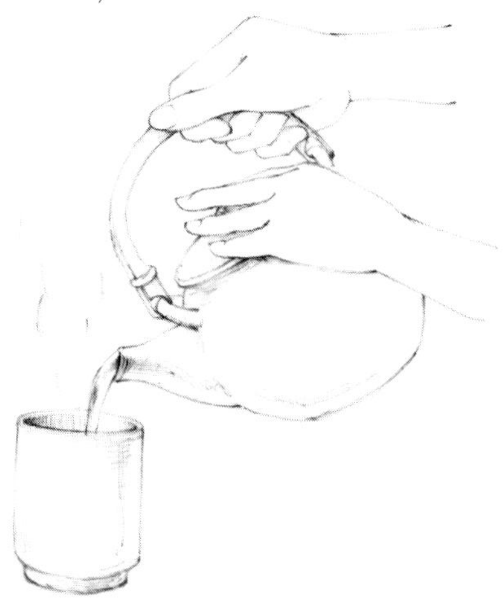

Teapots—that is, lidded and spouted pots used for making tea— do not have a long history, though, as stated above, similar pot forms have a very ancient history in Japan. Until the middle nineteenth century, tea drinking was not a custom of the average Japanese, but was practiced largely by the upper stratum of society. Generally, in a conventional household, after rice was eaten, boiling water was poured into the rice bowl and drunk as a beverage. For boiling this water, either an iron kettle (pages 59–63) or a ceramic kettle teapot was used. Even up until the end of the last war, tea drinking was not a common custom in northern Japan.

The use of decoration on the glazed body of the *bancha* teapots and the proliferation of decorative shapes is ample evidence of the relationship between the economy and the tea-drinking custom. A certain amount of leisure is necessary to be able to relax and enjoy tea after a meal. The ability to buy the tea must exist, as well as the ability to buy a decorated pot that serves to punctuate and, as it were, symbolize the enjoyment of this beverage and the economic level that permits this pleasure. The kettle teapots for boiling water are plain and austere; they reflect a frugal existence that did not allow the time or relaxed attention necessary to enjoy a decorated surface.

The pots on pages 18–29 are for the more expensive *sencha* tea. They may also be used for *bancha*. *Sencha* is high-quality tea and is largely reserved for serving to guests, not for everyday household use. Since the teapots used for *sencha* are placed before guests, these pots are highly decorative and refined.

On pages 20 bottom, 22, and 23 are shown examples of sets in which teapots and cups are designed as decorative accessories. Such sets are a relatively recent derivation from the more orthodox *sencha* sets centered around a *kyūsu* teapot (see below).

On pages 30 and 31 are pictured some eccentric teapot types. The pot on page 30, top, was originally used as a server for local distilled spirits (*shōchū*); recently it was adapted to teapot use and is sold today as a teapot. The pot on the middle of this page with the faceted body is the work of a contemporary artist-potter. It is an original design without direct traditional basis. The pot on the bottom of page 30 is ceramic, but it is a replica in glazed clay of a common Western metal tea kettle. Like its prototype, this pot was also used as a kettle; it is no longer made. The pots on page 31 are derived from an Anglo-Chinese pot form used for black tea. These are made at Mino for export to Europe, the Middle East, and Hawaii. The ones pictured have a brown slip-glaze; white ones are made for the Middle East.

Pages 32–35 reproduce a selection of modern and contemporary pots, all of which were purchased or borrowed to photograph for this book. This is a good cross-section of what is available in Japan, though designs and forms change with fashion. Such pots are sold in department stores, tea shops, aod ceramic ware shops, and some of the older ones (usually with cracks and scratches) in antique shops.

No detailed identifications of individual pots have been included here, because pot designs and shapes change relatively quickly. Even the older pots are no more than about eighty years old, but since they are "antiques," there is little certainty that they will be available to purchase.

Pots with upright handles are referred to as *dobin*. This handle once had the function of allowing the pot to hang over a fire. Pots without this standing handle are known as *kyūsu*. These are usually small and have a ceramic handle attached to the pot body at approximately a right angle to the spout. Some *kyūsu* have only an everted lip spout and no handle (pages 40, top; 41, top).

A *kyūsu* is held in the right hand. The fingers grip the handle, while the thumb is used to secure the lid (see sketch).

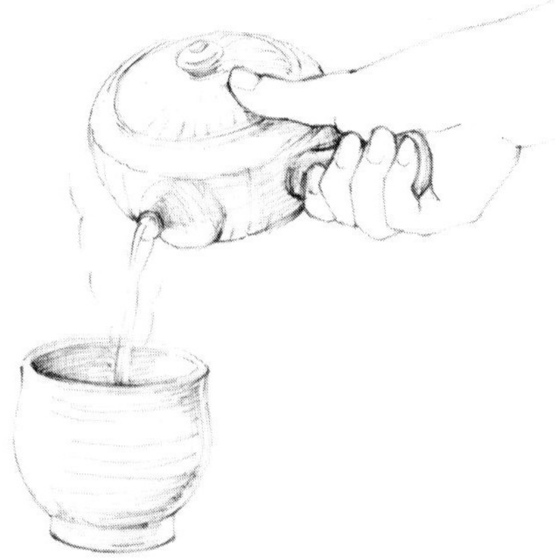

Dobin pots are large and are used to serve many people. *Kyūsu* are small and are used to serve either a few people or a single honored guest.

The tiny pots reflecting the *dobin* form are used as soy sauce servers (see page 64, bottom, and comments below).

Dobin and *kyūsu* are made throughout Japan. Because the popularity of porcelain pots has increased in recent years, Kyoto, the Arita area of Kyushu, Mino and Seto near Nagoya, and Aizu-Hongō in northern Japan (all major porcelain production areas) now make a large percentage of these pots.

The increased use of porcelain is a direct reflection of economic prosperity and continues a trend started in the early years of the nineteenth century. The whiteness and clarity of porcelain is sought for drinking and eating vessels; it is also associated with affluence. Ooe categosy of *kyūsu*, known popularly as Banko ware, is made of a fine, dense, red clay (see below).

The pots on pages 36–52 are a representative selection of *kyūsu*. Originally *kyūsu* were not for everyday use, but were used to serve quality teas, such as *sencha* and the costly *gyokuro*, to guests. Since the war, these pots have come to be more and more used for everyday purposes, another example of a luxury item becoming commonplace. As with *sencha dobin* teapots, *kyūsu* are small, the surface design and form are highly decorative and refined, and the price is high.

Sencha was drunk as early as the Muromachi period (1333–1573), roughly the same time as powdered tea ceremony tea was introduced. Of course, this custom was only an aristocratic pastime at first. The use of *sencha* in the Edo period (1615–1868) was limited largely to the area around and west of Kyoto, the area under the influence of the feudal lords who had close contact with the imperial court culture in Kyoto. These geographical boundaries of *sencha*'s popularity apply even today; *sencha* is still not as common in eastern and northern Japan as in western areas, where it is commonplace. This tea was also favored by literati of the eighteenth and nineteenth centuries.

Usually the *kyūsu* for *sencha* comes in a set, accompamied by five cups and a small vessel for cooling the hot water (*yu-zamashi*). Single *kyūsu* are available, but the set is more common (however, see Banko ware, below). The cups in such a set are tiny, usually about 1¼–1½ inches (3–4 centimeters) in diameter and height—only enough for a taste or two of tea (see page 46, bottom). While *bancha* defines the end of a meal, *sencha* has a strong social function. It appears when guests are entertained; a sip or two of *sencha* is enjoyed as a prelude to conversation. It has been likened by some to the role played by Turkish or Arabic coffee in the Middle East as an expression of hospitality.

Sencha is made as follows: boiling water is poured into the water-cooling vessel (at left in photograph, page 46, bottom). When the temperature is about 60–70°C, this water is poured onto the *sencha* leaves in the *kyūsu*, and the leaves are allowed to steep until the color is right. The *kyūsu* is then used to serve the tea. This is the proper procedure. (There is an elaborate *sencha* ceremony also, analogous to the more famous tea ceremony centered around powdered tea, but that is another subject.) Today, many people, either out of impatience or ignorance, pour boiling water directly onto the *sencha* leaves in the *kyūsu*. The reason for controlling the water temperature is to prepare a delicious beverage. Ignoring the nature of this tea by scalding the leaves with boiling water results in a slightly unpleasant drink. *Sencha kyūsu* sets are made largely at Hagi, Bizen, and Kyoto.

The angle formed by *kyūsu* spout and handle is important (see page 55). Usually this angle is between 90° and 100°, and it is this angle that allows a proper balance when the pot is held. A glance at the photographs shows that there are various shapes of handle and spout as well as pot body. Which is best depends entirely on the size and shape of the pourer's hand. It is not possible to say that any one handle or spout among the many commonly used is best in principle or in general. Of course, occasionally an artist-potter will produce a "new" design, which most often turns out to be unusable.

The *kyūsu* pictured on pages 47–51 are known as Banko ware and are the most widely used *kyūsu* in today's Japan. This type of ware is made of highly refined clay; it is unglazed and fires from a brick red to a purple-brown. The red clay has a high iron oxide content, while the purplish color has manganese. There are also buff (referred to in Japanese as "white") and green colors. Usually these pots are oxidation fired, but sometimes a reduction atmosphere is used at the end of firing to darken the color. Surfaces may be textured in various ways, have incised decoration, or be burnished, but the pots are never glazed.

Though these pots are made at many kilns throughout Japan, they are all referred to as Banko ware. The reasons for this are historical, and there seem to be many opinions concerning the origin of this ware in Japan. It does not seem to be of great antiquity, and today a large percentage is produced at Yokkaichi (supposedly the original home of Banko ware) and at Tokoname, south of Nagoya.

These *kyūsu* are mainly used for *bancha*, but may also be used for *sencha*. This is perhaps because they first spread throughout eastern Japan, where *bancha* was common but the *sencha* custom had oot yet beeo adopted. Though at the time of their introduction these Chinese-inspired pots were considered the height of rare luxury, today they are ubiquitous in eastern Japan and are obtainable wherever teapots are sold, including supermarkets.

Pages 56–63 illustrate a small selection of metal pots. The brass pots with copper trim on pages 56 and 57 are not teapots, but are water pitchers or ewers. (In fact, two of them have scorch marks on the bottom, indicating use over a direct flame. Some were indeed used as hot water kettles in this manner, placed on the charcoal fire of the type of heating brazier [*naga-hibachi*] characteristic of the area around Tokyo.)

Such brass pots came into use after the middle of the nineteenth century, largely in urban areas, and specifically in and around Tokyo. They were used simply as water pitchers and also to hold the water added to cool some types of tea.

The pewter pots on page 58 are small teapots. Pewter, of course, has too low a melting point to be used directly over a flame. Traditionally pewter was expensive in Japan and was used mainly by feudal lords and wealthy merchants, as well as in Shinto shrines and Buddhist temples. There was a limited Japanese pewter craft, but no real study has been made of this. The tin used to form this alloy, apparently, was imported.

For some reason, pewter seems to have been used mainly to form saké and tea utensils (both religious and profane). Such a little pewter pot would have been taken out of its special wooden box only for the purpose of entertaining a special guest or for some other special occasion. The shapes of these two pots are based on ceramic *dobin* teapot shapes.

The iron pots on pages 59–63 are tea kettles not teapots. They are cast iron and were and are made at only a few places in Japan. Today the area around Morioka in Iwate Prefecture is the main production center for cast ironware of this kind. Such kettles were suspended from a pot-hanger over a hearth fire or were placed on iron supports directly over a charcoal fire in a brazier.

The design of the pot on page 62, bottom, and on page 63 also allowed this type to be used on the traditional Japanese cookstove. The flange structure is functional and acted to contain the heat when the pot was on the stove, which was nothing more than a few holes in the top of an adobe (later brick) firebox, into which pots and kettles were set. This flanged form is decoratively reflected in the little Banko ware *kyūsu* on page 62 bottom and also in the iron kettle on page 60, top, in which a decorative relief pattern appears on the cast-iron surface. Iron kettles are no longer a part of everyday Japanese life; today they may be found in use mainly in a few rural households, in some Japanese inns, and in the homes of tea ceremony devotees. Still, they are decorative and pleasant objects, and the demand for them is still alive.

Iron kettles rust, but will remain rust free if kept full of simmering water over a low flame or a charcoal fire.

The objects on page 64 are related to teapots in various ways.

The little pots in a diagonal row at the top are train teapots. Such little ceramic pots hold a few swallows of tea, and at one time they were sold at railway station platforms and in trains throughout Japan. Shapes differed somewhat in different parts of Japan and at different times. The pots were simple, one-use throwaways; one invariably spilled hot tea on one's knees or over one's hands, but these little ceramic pots are remembered with great affection and nostalgia today. Pots of similar shape and size are still sold in stations and on trains, but these all are made of polyurethane or other plastics and come equipped with nonspill lips. The pot at the far right is one of the earlier plastic forms; this is no longer made today.

These little train pots were the bread-and-butter ware of many local kilns, but particularly large numbers were made at Tachikui (Tamba) and at Mashiko. The little lid was the cup; the content of the pot was about $6\frac{1}{2}$ ounces (200 milliliters).

The lidded teapotlike vessel in the middle of the page is a special pot for cooking and serving the dish known as *dobin mushi*. The main ingredient of this is mushrooms, and it is a fancy descendant of the type of simple mushroom cookery described in the first section on kettle teapots. This vessel, however, has no other use than to make this dish, and is an object one is more likely to encounter in a restaurant than in a private home, though they are often sold in department stores and in ceramic stores. This vessel has kept the teapot form, but it is nonfunctional—the pot is placed in a steamer to cook the contents.

The small pots at the bottom of the page, derived from *dobin* shapes, are soy sauce servers. They are strictly a postwar phenomenon and are a reflection of the postwar prosperity that allowed such whimsies. They are for decorative table use, and are present when soy sauce plays an important role in the meal. This may be every meal or only when such things as sushi are served.

Some readers might wonder why no mention has been made of the utensils used in the famous Japanese tea ceremony. The simple reason is that this book is limited to teapots and related forms, and no such objects are used in the tea ceremony. The tea ceremony has a complex culture of its own and has been the subject of numerous books.

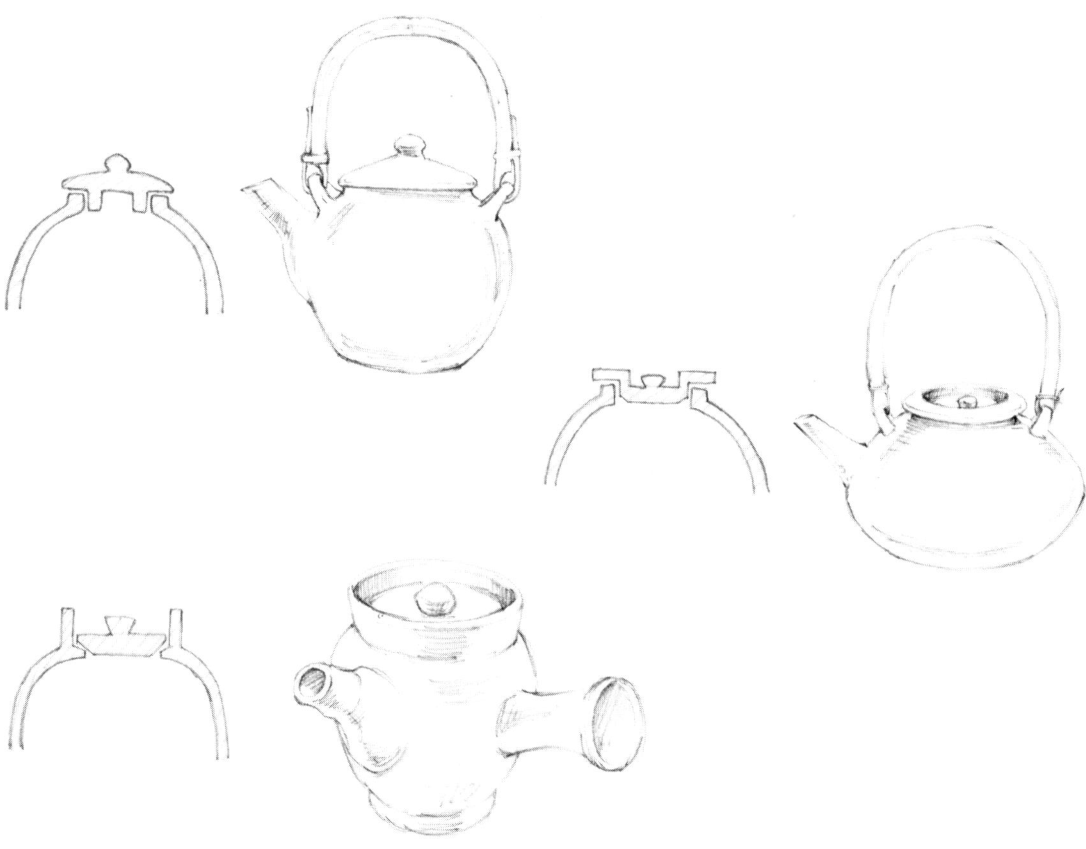

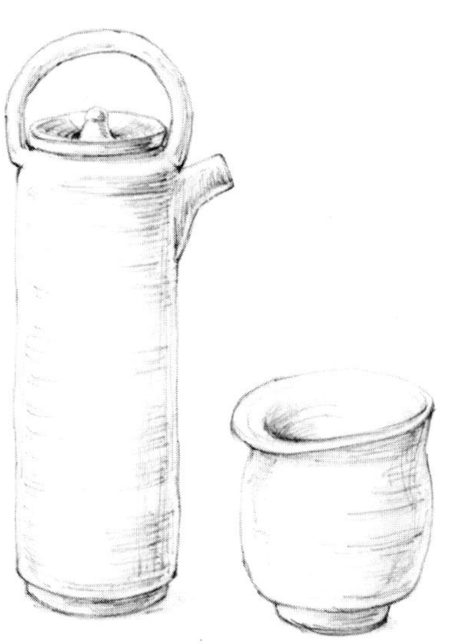

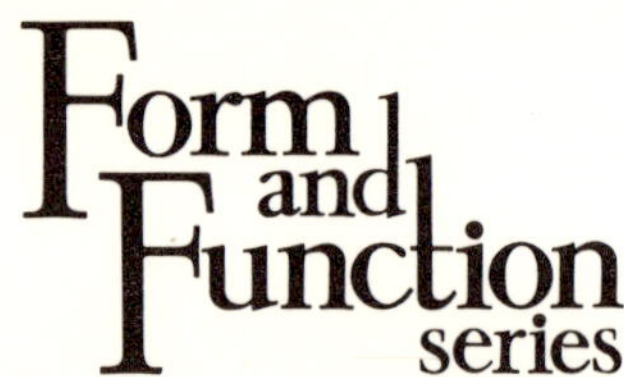

the beauty of everyday objects

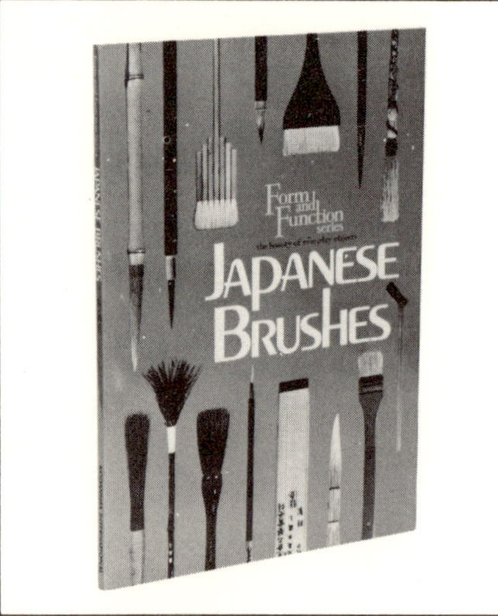

Japanese Brushes

Introduction and Photographs by Masao Usui

The influence of the brush on Japanese culture cannot be overemphasized. Today it still holds pride of place in the respect and affections of the Japanese in spite of cheaper, mass-produced writing tools. The *fude* of the artist and the *hake* of the artisan, as demonstrated here, both exhibit the same technical prowess and sensitivity toward materials that is the hallmark of Japanese craftsmanship.

ISBN 0-87011-370-4 80 pp. $8.95

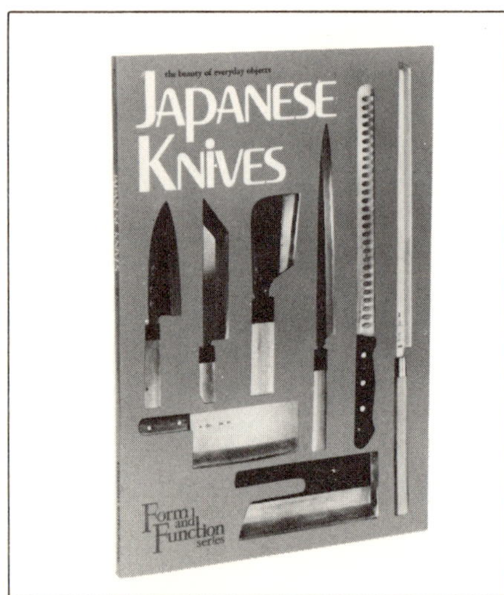

Japanese Knives

Introduction by Yoshio Akioka
Photographs by Masao Usui

There are still many smiths in Japan today who hand-fashion various types of cutlery, employing unique techniques essentially unchanged for the past hundred years. The craftsman's strong, almost imperative sense that a tool must match the job remains very much alive in the fine-quality chisels, utility knives, and kitchen knives imaginatively photographed in this volume.

ISBN 0-87011-371-2 79 pp. $8.95

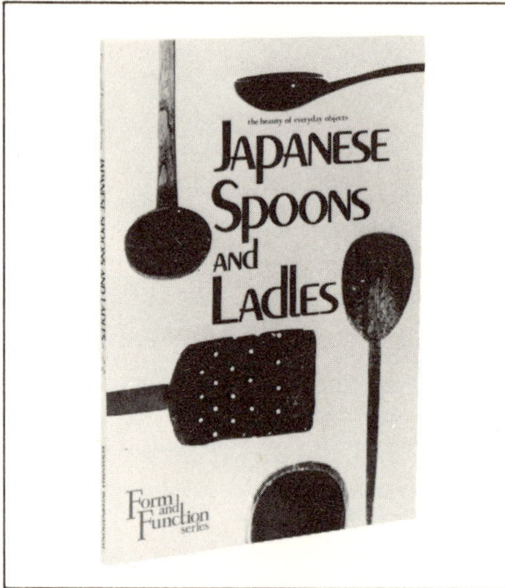

Japanese Spoons and Ladles

Introduction by Yoshio Akioka
Photographs by Masao Usui

Wooden objects permeate all aspects of daily life in Japan—from the houses made of wood to the wooden utensils used in the home—and reflect the wood culture which evolved early in its history. The spoons, scoops, and ladles exhibited here have been skillfully sculpted from different varieties of trees into highly functional as well as aesthetic objects.

ISBN 0-87011-372-0 78 pp. $8.95

Forthcoming titles:

Japanese Teapots

Japanese Boxes